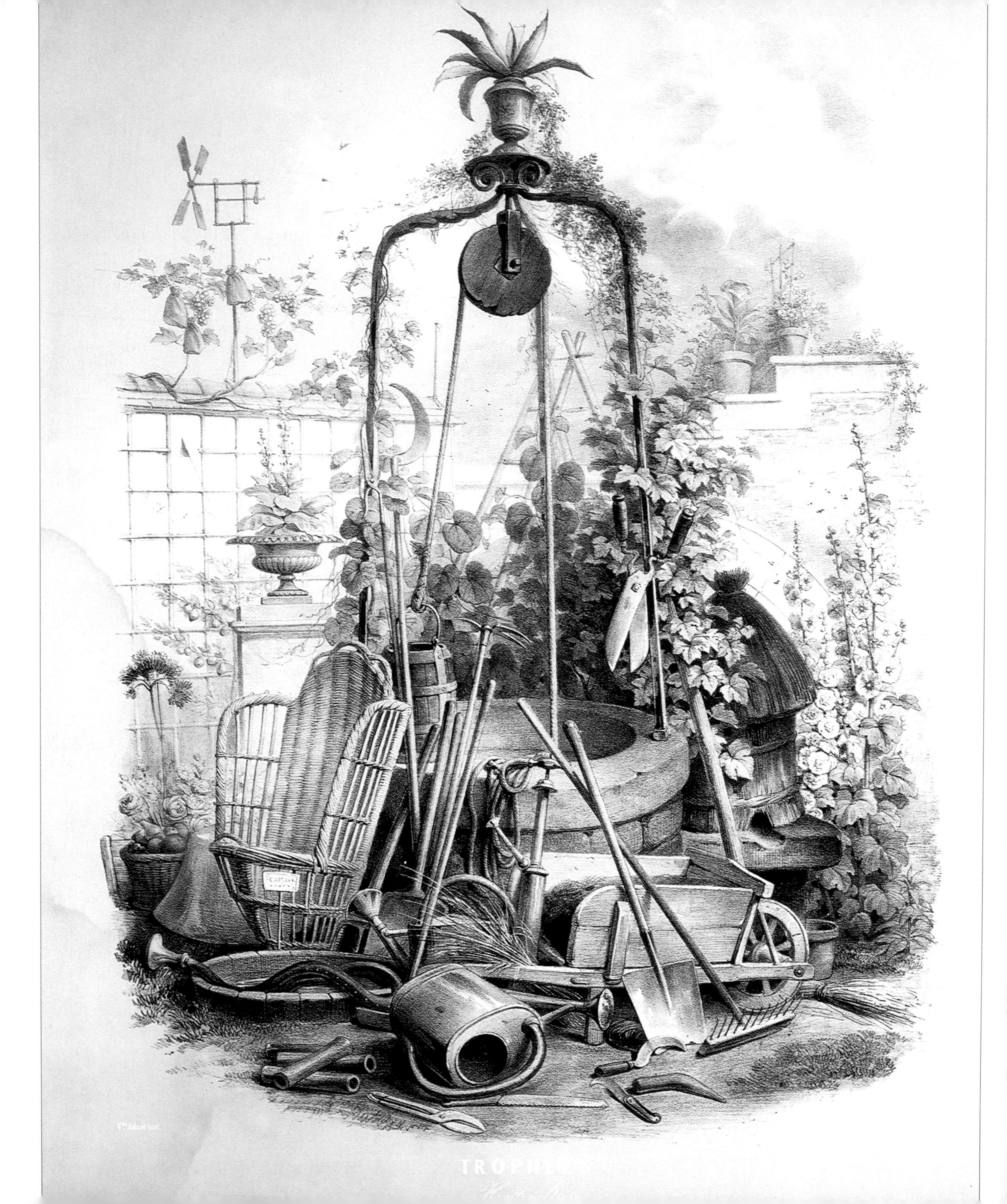

EVERYDAY THINGS™
GARDEN TOOLS

EVERYDAY THINGS™

GARDEN TOOLS

SUZANNE SLESIN

GUILLAUME PELLERIN

STAFFORD CLIFF

DANIEL ROZENSZTROCH

LOCATION PHOTOGRAPHS: BERNARD TOUILLON

STYLIST: ALIX DE DIVES

STUDIO PHOTOGRAPHS: MARC SCHWARTZ

TEXT

SUZANNE SLESIN & GUILLAUME PELLERIN

DESIGN

STAFFORD CLIFF

ABBEVILLE PRESS

PUBLISHERS

NEW YORK • LONDON • PARIS

Editor: Jacqueline Decter
Art Director: Patricia Fabricant
Production Editor: Owen Dugan
Production Manager: Lou Bilka

Library of Congress
Cataloging-in-Publication
Data
Slesin, Suzanne.
Garden tools / Suzanne
Slesin . . . [et al.].
p. cm. —
(Everyday things)
Includes bibliographical
references and index.
ISBN 0-7892-0087-2
1. Garden tools. 2. Gardening—Equipment
and supplies. I. Title.
II. Series.
SB454.8.S58 1996
681′.7631—dc20
95-44910

Jacket front: Typical late-nineteenth-century zinc and iron watering cans (see also page 97).
Jacket back: An array of gardening paraphernalia fills the attic of a nineteenth-century barn (see also page 8).
Endpapers: "The Gardener," toile de Jouy, c. 1770.
Facing half-title page: A late-nineteenth-century lithograph by Frenchman Victor Adam offers a romantic interpretation of rural pursuits.
Half-title page: An eighteenth-century copper watering can has a reinforced base and double handle.
Frontispiece: Tole and wood fruit pickers, mainly nineteenth century, fill a wicker basket.
Page 4: A 1940s jigsaw puzzle made of blocks on a garden theme is still in its original box.

Inquiries should be addressed to Abbeville Publishing Group, 22 Cortlandt Street, New York, N.Y. 10007. The text of this book was set in Syntax and Bodoni Book. Printed and bound in Hong Kong.

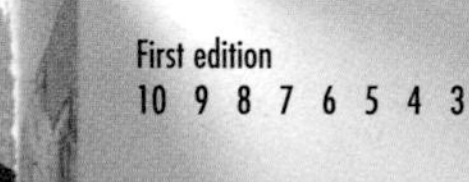

First edition
10 9 8 7 6 5 4 3

8
PREFACE
13
HISTORY
29
PREPARING
THE EARTH
43
SOWING
AND PLANTING
59
NURTURING
AND PROTECTING
71
DEALING
WITH PESTS
83
WATERING
99
PRUNING
117
HARVESTING
135
MOWING AND
TRIMMING
154
DIRECTORY
BIBLIOGRAPHY
ACKNOWLEDGMENTS
INDEX

A ten-acre garden requires a large number and range of tools for year-round maintenance by two full-time gardeners. Spades, forks, hoes, a seeder, and a scythe are among the many tools neatly stored in a rack designed by the proprietor of the garden and made by the local carpenter.

LE PAYSAN

PREFACE

On a mild December day in 1994 we took a train from Paris to Cherbourg to see Guillaume Pellerin's collection of garden tools in their natural habitat—his family's home, a stone castle with a panoramic view of the ocean on one of the northernmost tips of France. We expected to be ushered into a museumlike environment, with watering cans, seed boxes, rakes, and cloches set out carefully, ready to be admired as the relics of a craft and culture that is no more. Instead we found a well-lived-in house and tools everywhere: trowels and pruners by the dozens, fruit pickers in baskets, watering cans at the bottom of the stairs, sprayers on shelves in the attic, and shovels and spades crammed into a shed. The bookcase in the library was bursting with seed and garden catalogs. In one of the bedrooms large advertising posters for fertilizer were lovingly stored flat, some underneath the bed. We found ourselves under the spell of a collection that was a living, changing, growing organism. And a collector who appreciated and knew every item by name.

Guillaume Pellerin's passion for garden tools began when, as a child in Normandy, France, he saw a family friend's array of tools. "They were all so well laid out, so impeccably kept," Pellerin recalled more than thirty-five years later, himself now the proud owner of more than four thousand hand-made tools and one of the most knowledgeable specialists in a field that has long been overlooked.

LEFT In the attic of a nineteenth-century barn, an amazing array of gardening paraphernalia has accumulated. Willow harvest baskets, wooden boxes, flower troughs, and a seed display rack are piled high behind dozens of tools.

Pellerin's interest in the tools used to nurture and maintain a garden is inextricably linked to his love for the ten-acre garden that surrounds the Château de Vauville, a twelfth-century stone castle on the coast of Normandy, near Cherbourg. The property has been in his family for more than a hundred years. The youngest of seven children, Pellerin, along with his sister Marie-Noëlle (she is three years older), "grew up in the garden."

The present garden—created in 1947 by Pellerin's father, Eric, for his mother, Nicole—is a special place. The plants—most of which remain green all year long—came from the Southern hemisphere, and were meant to create the atmosphere of a sunny climate to counteract the region's perennially overcast skies. "It was a garden to dream in," says Pellerin.

As the garden took shape over the years, Pellerin would follow his father around, observing, studying, and appreciating every plant and every tool. After the death of his parents, Pellerin and his sister "were the only ones to speak up for the garden." It was a rather large responsibility to take on, as by then the garden had been registered as a historic landmark, and its rare and unusual plants required year-round attention. "When we decided to take it on, we were either unconscious or in love," says Pellerin. Or both.

Pellerin's collection of tools had grown by that time,

too. He had been a collector, probably without knowing it, ever since he was a small boy and enjoyed accompanying his mother to flea markets in Paris. "I see myself holding her hand, stopping to buy something that caught my eye," he recalls.

He understood early on that each tool had its own specific function, and that garden tools were entitled to the same care and respect as the tools of other crafts. "I began to see garden tools as friends, rather than symbols of hard work," he says.

The moment that galvanized Pellerin's search for old tools was the sight, years ago, of a ship piled high with scrap metal on its way from Normandy to Japan, where the discarded material would be "transformed into Toyotas." Pellerin began energetically frequenting flea markets, foraging through the piles of old metal bits, broken tools, and scrap—all the stuff that "people didn't want anymore"—to come up with his treasures: trowels, spades, dibbers, clippers, and pruners, all remnants of the hand-forged tools, the everyday things, that had once had purposeful lives but had been thrown away or left to rust because they were broken or just not needed anymore. The cut-off date of Pellerin's collection is about 1950, when garden tools became widely mass-produced. "After that there are no more errors or imprints of the human hand," he says. "That's when I lose interest."

In Pellerin's mind, the beauty of garden tools is inseparable from the craft of the gardener who toiled throughout the year, inventing, refining, and adapting the tools that were extensions of his hands, helping him create, mold, and nurture the plantings that were to flourish and become part of the garden landscape. Yet for centuries the gardener was not accorded the respect that Pellerin believed was his due. "If a person failed at school," he says, "his family brought him home, saying, 'Oh, never mind, he'll just work in the garden.'" That was all wrong. "Gardening is a craft that requires having a sense of both art and tradition. You can never know enough to make a garden. You have to be a painter to achieve a balanced color palette, a sculptor to discern the volumes, an architect to determine the organization and master plan, and an engineer to figure out the distribution of water without which a garden cannot flourish. But maybe most important, you must be a poet. That's because the garden has to have a soul."

And like the generations of gardeners before you, you will definitely need the right tools.

RIGHT Two nineteenth-century wooden wheelbarrows have now been retired to a barn attic. The one in the foreground was for transporting bundles of hay or freshly cut grass. The other was often used to cart wet laundry from the local washhouse.

HISTORY

For thousands of years gardening has ensured the survival of the human race and affirmed our mastery over our living environment. A garden can represent anything from an idealized vision of Eden to a means of gratifying scientific curiosity, from an indication of social standing to a creation meant solely for private pleasure. Fragile and ephemeral architecture though they may be, gardens are nevertheless constant witnesses to the scientific and technical advances of the human adventure. The sensual pleasures of gardens have been described by King Solomon in the Bible, by Semiramis, the legendary creator of the hanging gardens of Babylon, and by ancient Chinese and Indian poets. Centuries ago voyagers were dazzled by the famous gardens of the kings of Persia and the caliphs of Baghdad. From Egypt to Mexico, from Greece to China, gardens have always been an intrinsic part of the world's great civilizations. And the story of garden tools is inseparable from the history of gardens.

Yet, while the history of gardens has been explored and recorded in detail since antiquity, the origin and evolution of garden tools have been virtually ignored. The Latin author Columella and the Roman naturalist Pliny the Elder, who questioned not only the whys but the hows of gardening, are nearly unique in their writings. Hidden behind familiar, everyday tools is a rich history that documents the tastes and passions of gardeners through the ages.

The first representations of tools for working the soil—dibbers made from the ribs of mammoths—can be found in Paleolithic cave paintings in France dating back to 40000 B.C. Tools are also depicted in ancient Egyptian wall reliefs and medieval illuminated manuscripts. Man developed the tools necessary for cultivation with the same ingenuity that gave shape to weapons for hunting and fighting. The hunting lance topped by a rock or carved piece of bone would become a dibber and primitive hoe. The earliest extant remnants of garden tools date back to the Neolithic period (from 8000 to 1500 B.C.). Dibbers with triangular stone heads dating back to 5000 B.C. were unearthed in Mesopotamia. The predynastic Egyptians fashioned hoes by tying a V-shaped branch to a thick piece of wood. The Greeks had many cultivating tools, including toothed hoes, picking hooks, rakes, and shovels, and the Romans expanded the use of metal for reinforcing or replacing wood.

In the tenth and eleventh centuries A.D., the Crusaders in the Middle East brought back to Europe not only new varieties of plants, such as lilac, hyacinth, and ranunculus, but also innovative irrigation techniques. During the Middle Ages gardening tools were for the most part crafted of wood, bone, horn, and stone, but the use of iron, reserved since Roman times for making weapons, improved their quality and durability. Iron tools were forged by the blacksmith-craftsman,

LEFT *Spring*, a late-sixteenth-century painting by Abel Grimmer, probably after Pieter Brueghel the Younger, illustrates in minute detail the gardening tools and sophisticated techniques already in use at the time. Musée des Beaux-Arts, Lille.

who was also the maker of arms; even when tools designated for gardening became separate from farming equipment and weapons, they were still made by blacksmiths.

The Renaissance ushered in a new conception of the art of living, and garden tools began to be rendered with greater sophistication. In the second half of the sixteenth century, during the reign of Henry IV, studies led to lighter, more efficient arms and tools. More refined tools were developed for the women who took care of the household chores while men were at war or working away in the fields.

Eleven tools are described in Englishman Leonard Mascall's book on gardening (1572); Frenchman Olivier de Serres's famous *Mesnage des champs* (1603) cites ten; the German Petrus Laurenberg's *Horticultura* (1631) lists thirty-five; and Englishman John Evelyn's *Elysium Brittanicum* (1659)—the most complete survey of its time—illustrates more than seventy tools. One indication of the importance accorded these ordinary objects during the Renaissance is that they would often be blessed along with farm animals in the hope of providing a bountiful harvest.

The seventeenth century, with its passion for horticulture, saw the proliferation of specialized tools for precise tasks. Before the Industrial Revolution, the majority of tools were custom-made by the local blacksmith, who would craft each tool to the strength and size of a gardener's hands. Because iron was expensive and hard to find, it was a common practice to melt down the metal from broken tools and use it in new ones. Gardeners took great care of their tools, repairing them as necessary. Some were ornamented: hearts were a favored decoration, as were religious mottos and vegetal designs, including leaves, flowers, and scrolls.

With the expansion of trade to the New World and the geographic expeditions of the eighteenth century, new tools and equipment—fern knives, orchid pots, cactus clippers, and pineapple packing cases, to name a few—were invented to assist in the cultivation of plants that had been unknown in Europe until that time. After the French Revolution professional gardeners would often travel from place to place. They required two types of tools: those that remained in the garden, such as wheelbarrows, carts, ladders, and water barrels, and the portable variety, including pruners, trowels, shears, saws, knives, and dibbers, which the gardener carried with him in a kit or box.

Mass production of garden tools began at the beginning of the nineteenth century in response to the demands of the growing middle class, for whom gardening was a favorite leisure pursuit. Peugeot established a tool factory in the town of St. Etienne, France, in 1810, but the most important factory in Europe was to be Goldenberg, in Alsace, which is still in operation today. By 1900 mail-order catalogs were filled with offers for tools in a great variety of shapes and sizes. But this trend would prove too costly for mass production, and only the best-selling tools would survive into the twentieth century.

Within a few decades the invention of small engines, the widespread use of electricity, and the growth in the use of chemical compounds made possible mechanization of almost every wearisome garden chore, relegating the extraordinary tools that had taken thousands of years to perfect to the realm of mere accessories. But today many of these basic, ordinary tools are being rediscovered, appreciated now as much for their ingenuity as for their timeless, sculptural forms.

RIGHT A mid-eighteenth-century engraving of a landscape designer overseeing the execution of his plans. Among the tools pictured are a leveler on the right, a watering can, and a rake. The importance of tree shaping can be seen.

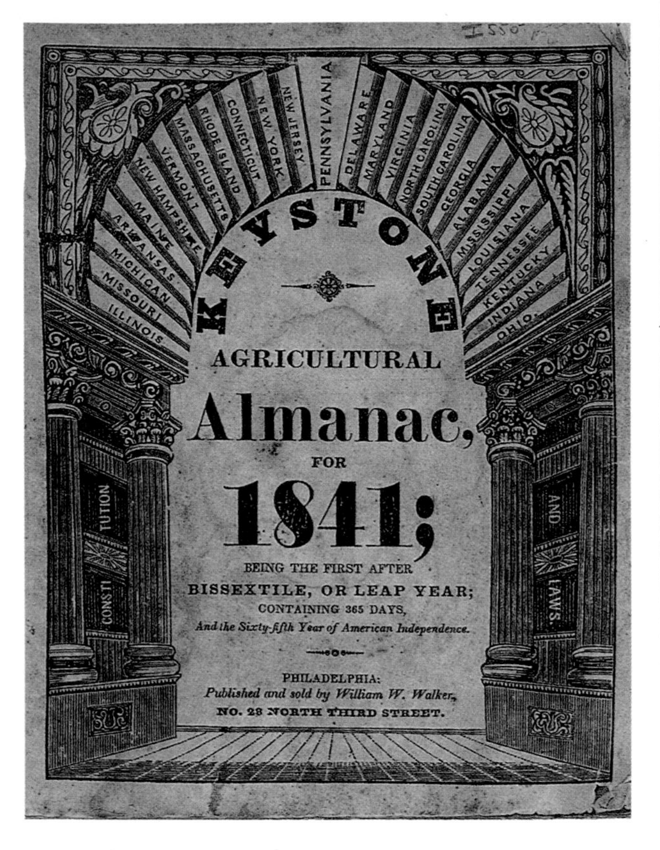

ABOVE Cover of one of the first agricultural almanacs distributed by hawkers to American farmers.

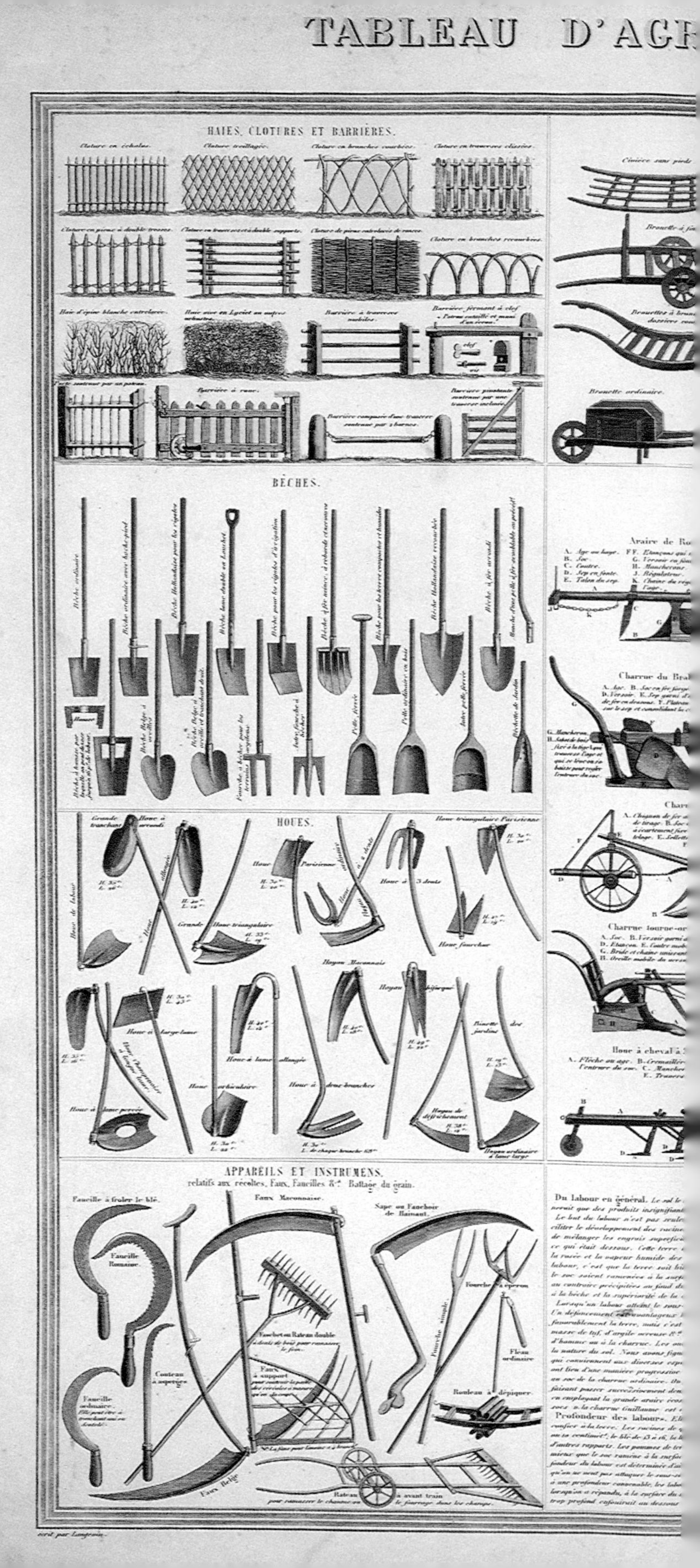

RIGHT This late-nineteenth-century colored lithograph depicting traditional farm and garden equipment served as a classroom chart. The illustrations were based on Denis Diderot's and Jean Le Rond d'Alembert's 1802 gardening encyclopedia and Pierre Boitard's ambitious and complete 1833 work on the implements of husbandry.

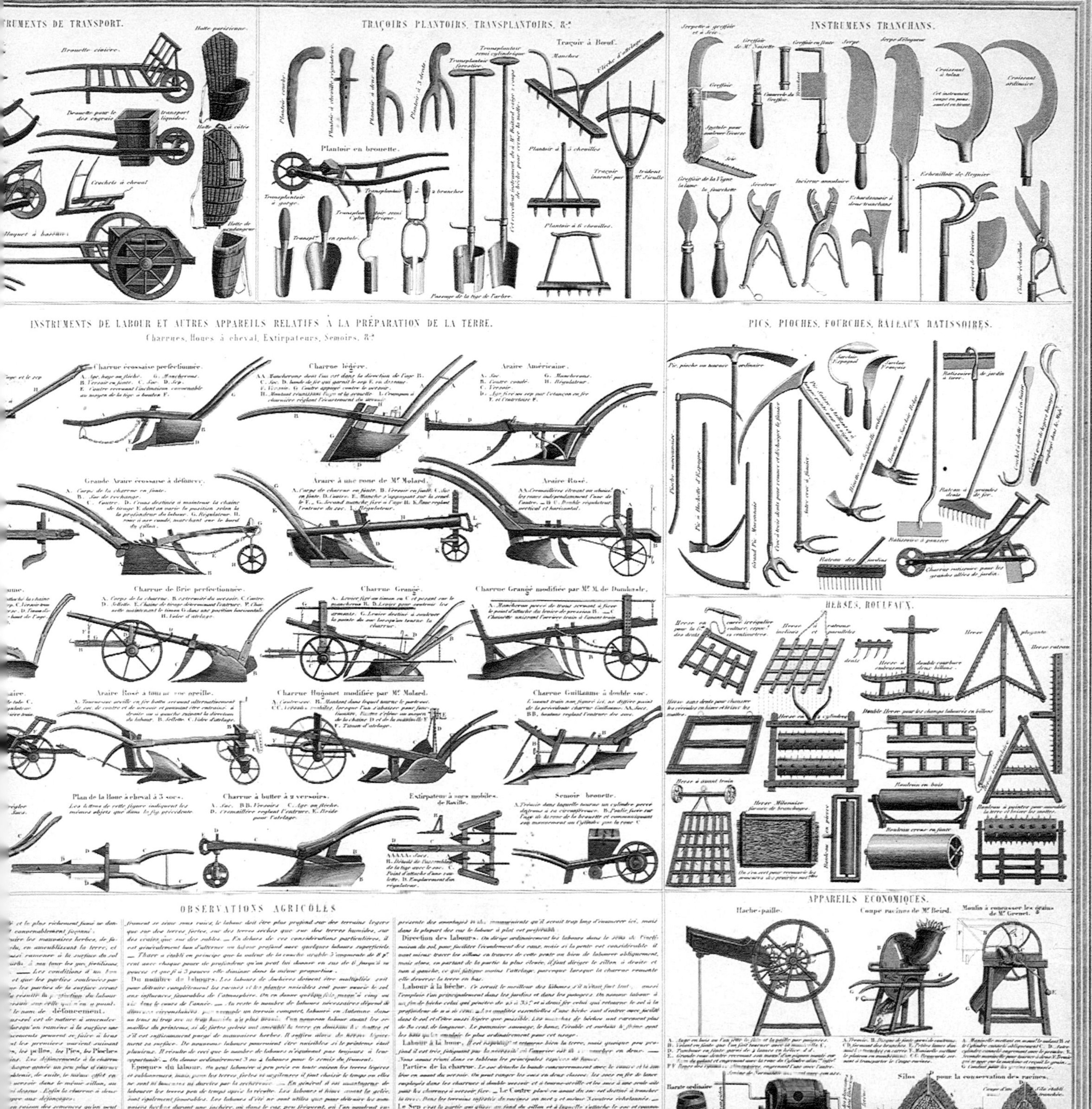

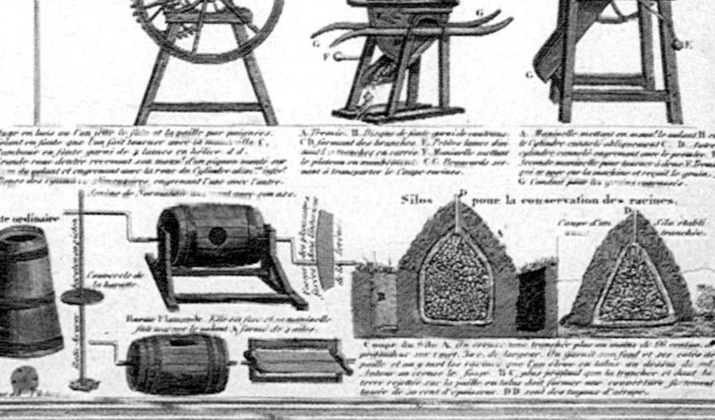

OBSERVATIONS AGRICOLES

... et le plus richement fumé ne don... convenablement façonné.
...uire les mauvaises herbes, de fa...lu, en ameublissant la terre, et ...ssi ramener à la surface du sol ...ués à son tour les gaz fertilisans. — Les conditions d'un bon ... et que les parties soulevées par ...e les parties de la surface seront ...le résultat du [illegible] du labour ...ssant avec celle qui n'en a point. ...le nom de **défoncement.**
...us-sol est de nature à amender ...lorsqu'on ramène à la surface une ...cements peuvent se faire à bras ...t les premiers varient suivant ...s, les **pelles, les Pics, les Pioches** ...ins. Les défoncements à la charrue ...chaque année un peu plus et entraîner ...obtenir, de suite, le même effet en ... versoir dans le même sillon, au ...i dessus. Enfin la charrue à deux ...pre aux défonçages.
...en raison des semences qu'on veut ...tes potagères ne pénètrent qu'à 8 ...à 48. Elle doit encore varier sous ...les fèves réussissent d'autant ...quantité de terre meuble. — La pro... de la terre arable, toutes les fois ...[illegible] a été labouré et ameubli ...rement être plus superficiels [illegible] ...tenons un engrais qu'un labour ...des racines. — Dans les pays où le froment se sème sous raies, le labour doit être plus profond sur des terrains légers que sur des terres fortes, sur des terres sèches que sur des terres humides, sur des craies que sur des sables. — En dehors de ces considérations particulières, il est généralement bon d'alterner un labour profond avec quelques labours superficiels. — Thaer a établi en principe que la valeur de la couche arable s'augmente de 8 p.% avec chaque pouce de profondeur qu'on peut lui donner en sus de 6 jusqu'à 10 pouces et que si à 3 pouces elle diminue dans la même proportion.

Du nombre des labours. Les labours de Jachères doivent être multipliés soit pour détruire complètement les racines et les plantes nuisibles soit pour ouvrir le sol aux influences favorables de l'atmosphère. On en donne quelquefois jusqu'à cinq ou six dans le cours de l'année. — Au reste le nombre de labours nécessaires dépend de diverses circonstances, par exemple un terrain compact, labouré en Automne dans un temps ni trop sec ni trop humide n'a plus besoin d'un nouveau labour avant les semailles du printems, si de fortes gelées ont ameubli la terre en divisant les mottes et s'il est suffisamment purgé de mauvaises herbes. Il suffira alors de herser légèrement sa surface. De nouveaux labours pourraient être nuisibles si le printems était pluvieux. Il résulte de ceci que le nombre de labours n'équivaut pas toujours à leur opportunité. — On donne ordinairement 3 ou 4 labours pour le semis du froment.

Epoques du labour. On peut labourer à peu près en toute saison les terres légères et sablonneuses, mais pour les terres fortes et argileuses il faut choisir le temps où elles ne sont ni boueuses ni durcies par la sècheresse. — En général il est avantageux de labourer les terres peu de temps après la récolte. Les labours d'hiver avant la gelée, sont également favorables. Les labours d'été ne sont utiles que pour détruire les mauvaises herbes durant une jachère, ou dans le cas, peu fréquent, où l'on voudrait ensemencer de nouveau une terre qui vient de donner une récolte.

De la manière de labourer. La largeur et l'épaisseur de la bande à soulever par le soc varie selon la nature du sol. Cette bande doit être plus étroite dans un sol tenace afin de faciliter l'action de la herse. Cependant avec six ou huit pouces d'entrure, on peut, dans cette nature de sol donner jusqu'à 9 ou 10 pouces de largeur à la raie. Si la largeur est beaucoup plus grande la tranche soulevée retombe à plat; dans le cas contraire elle s'incline seulement sur la couche précédente et laisse une de ses arêtes en l'air. Ce dernier mode est préféré par les agronomes.

On laboure un terrain à plat en planches ou en billons ou à dos. L'usage des billons présente des avantages et des inconvénients qu'il serait trop long d'énumérer ici, mais dans la plupart des cas le labour à plat est préférable.

Direction des labours. On dirige ordinairement les labours dans le sens de l'inclinaison du sol, pour faciliter l'écoulement des eaux, mais si la pente est considérable il vaut mieux tracer les sillons en travers de cette pente ou bien de labourer obliquement, mais alors, en partant de la partie la plus élevée, il faut diriger le sillon à droite et non à gauche, ce qui fatigue moins l'attelage, parceque lorsque la charrue remonte elle déverse la terre en bas.

Labour à la bêche. Ce serait le meilleur des labours s'il n'était fort lent, aussi l'emploie-t-on principalement dans les jardins et dans les potagers. On nomme labour à un fer de bêche celui qui pénètre de 25 à 35 c. et à demi fer celui qui retourne le sol à la profondeur de 12 à 16 cent. — Les qualités essentielles d'une bêche sont d'entrer avec facilité dans le sol et d'être aussi légère que possible. Les manches de bêches ont rarement plus de 80 cent. de longueur. Le pommier sauvage, le hêtre, l'érable et surtout le frêne sont les bois qu'on emploie le plus ordinairement pour cet usage.

Labour à la houe. Il est expéditif et retourne bien la terre, mais quoique peu profond il est très fatigant par la nécessité où l'ouvrier est de se courber en deux. — Nous avons réuni dans ce tableau les principales espèces de houes.

Parties de la charrue. Le soc détache la bande concurremment avec le coutre et la soulève en avant du versoir. On peut ranger les socs en deux classes: les socs en fer de lance employés dans les charrues à double versoir et à tourne-oreille et les socs à une seule aile pour les charrues à versoir fixe. — **Le Coutre** placé en avant du soc est destiné à trancher la terre. Dans les terrains infestés de racines on met 2 et même 3 coutres échelonnés. — **Le Sep** c'est la partie qui glisse au fond du sillon et à laquelle s'attache le soc et communément les manches. — **Le Versoir** retourne la terre que le soc a soulevé. Il est plane ou contourné. Ce dernier est bien préférable. Les meilleurs versoirs sont en fer ou en fonte. — **L'age ou la Flèche** est la partie par laquelle se transmet tout le mouvement. — **Les Mancherons.** Quelques charrues n'ont qu'un seul mancheron, mais celles à deux mancherons sont plus faciles à diriger. — **Le Régulateur** est un appareil de forme très variée servant à régler l'entrure de la charrue et même à modifier la largeur de la raie. Les charrues à avant-train prennent plus d'entrure quand on abaisse l'age sur la sellette. Les araires, ou charrues sans avant train piquent d'autant plus qu'on élève le point de tirage et vice versa.

19, Rue du Fg. S.t Jacques, Imprimé par Fessart

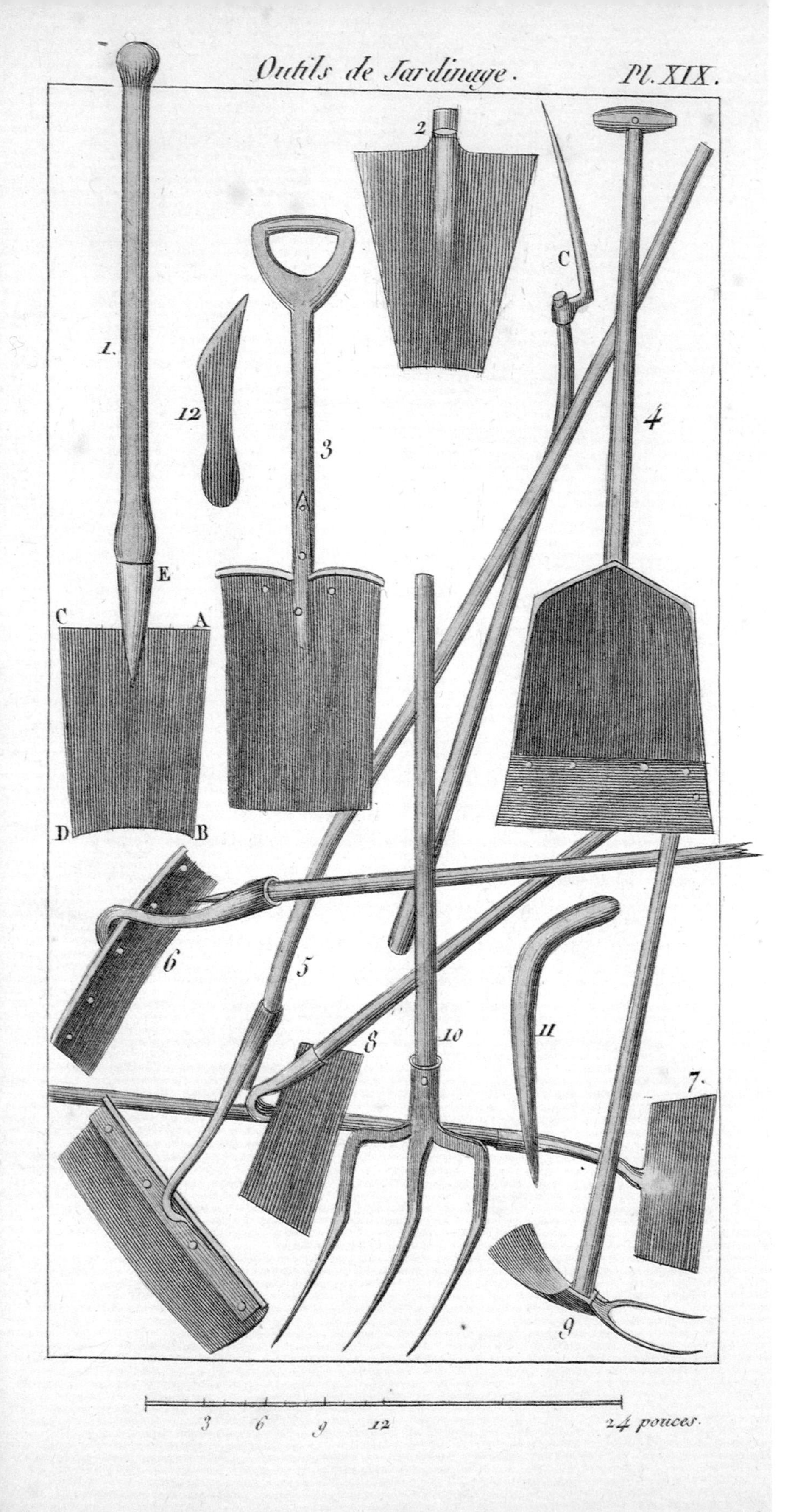

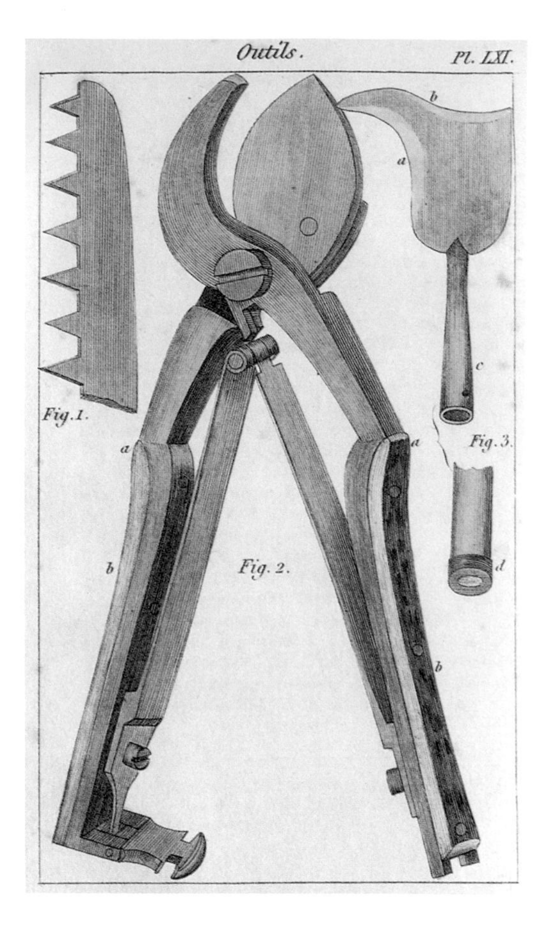

ABOVE An illustration, c. 1830, of a prototype of a pruner that uses the flexibility of metal as a spring. Its handle is covered in wood or stag horn. To its left is a detail of the teeth of a metal pruning saw. On the right is a blade for trimming low branches.

LEFT An eighteenth-century illustration showing the tools necessary for the maintenance of walks.

RIGHT A collection of French porcelain plates from such factories as Creil et Montereau and Choisy-le-Roi, all decorated with scenes depicting the gardener with his tools or landowners in their private gardens. Popular from the end of the eighteenth century on, antique plates with garden themes are now highly collectible rarities.

SEPTEMBRE
BALIVERNES RUSTIQUES

LES PARISIENS À LA CAMPAGNE
JARDINIÈRE
FLEURISTE

OU EST LE JARDINIER ?
LE JARDINIER
NOVEMBRE

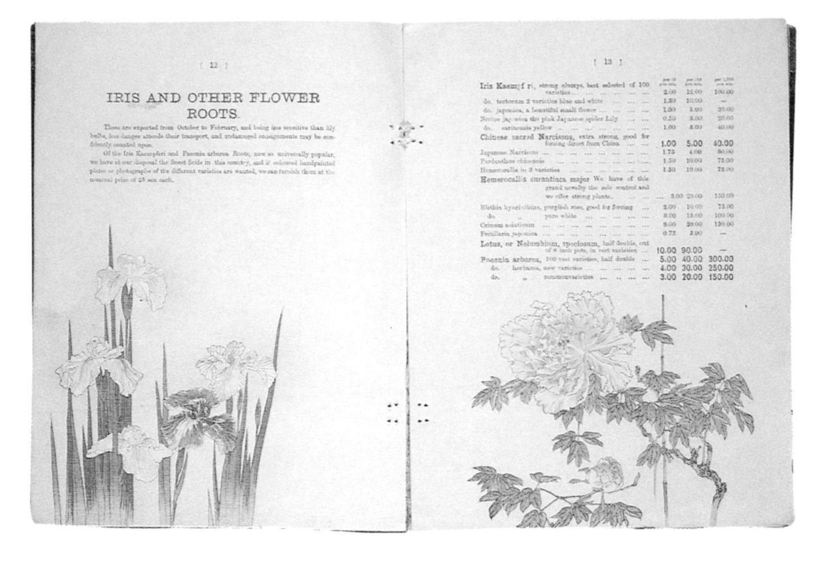

IRIS AND OTHER FLOWER ROOTS.

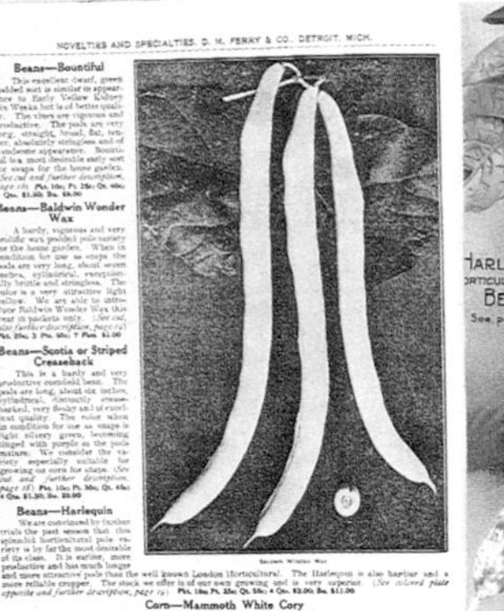

NOVELTIES AND SPECIALTIES. D. M. FERRY & CO. DETROIT, MICH.

Beans—Bountiful

Beans—Baldwin Wonder Wax

Beans—Scotia or Striped Creaseback

Beans—Harlequin

Corn—Mammoth White Cory

Corn—Avon Evergreen

JOHN A. SALZER SEED CO., LA CROSSE, WIS.

1924

SOW SALZER'S SEEDS

HOLLYHOCK

ICE PLANT—A

KOCHIA (SUMMER CYPRESS)—A

LANTANA HYBRIDA—P

LARKSPUR—A

LATHYRUS LATIFOLIUS (Perennial Pea)

LUPINS—A

LOBELIA—A

LEFT AND RIGHT European and American mail-order catalogs for seeds, tools, and other gardening equipment proliferated from 1850 on. Often printed in lavish color, the catalogs were an efficient way for people who lived in isolated areas to obtain up-to-date tools and new varieties of seeds every year. Catalogs diminished in popularity only at the time of World War II.

PUBLICATIONS PÉRIODIQUES DE LA MAISON VILMORIN-ANDRIEUX & Cie
N°1. 1er Janvier 1893
1893
CATALOGUE GÉNÉRAL
DE
GRAINES
FRAISIERS
Ognons à Fleurs
Etc.
VILMORIN-ANDRIEUX & Cie
Marchands-Grainiers
4, QUAI DE LA MÉGISSERIE, 4
PARIS

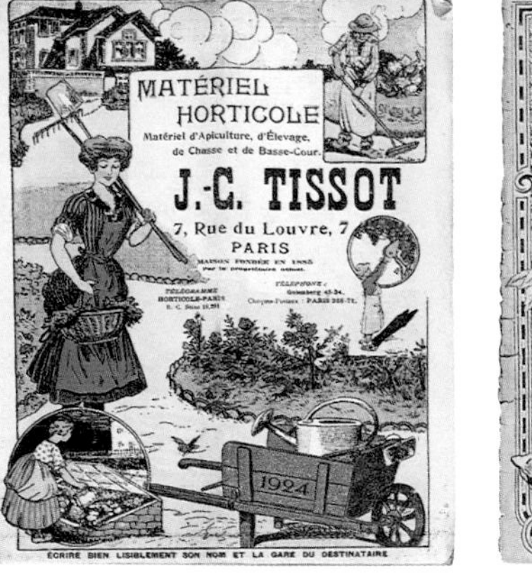
MATÉRIEL HORTICOLE
Matériel d'Apiculture, d'Élevage, de Chasse et de Basse-Cour
J.-C. TISSOT
7, Rue du Louvre, 7
PARIS
1924
ÉCRIRE BIEN LISIBLEMENT SON NOM ET LA GARE DU DESTINATAIRE

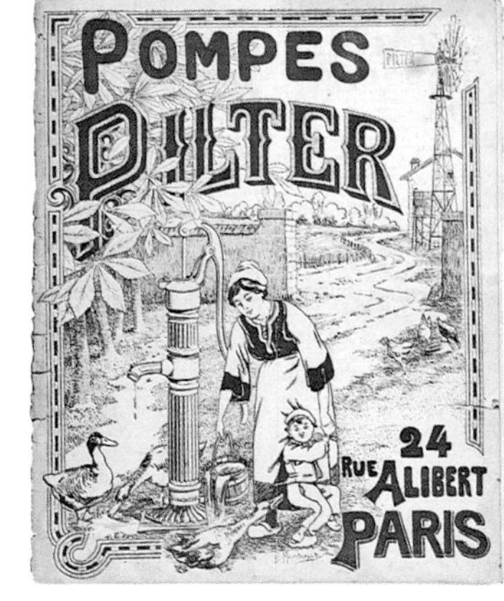
POMPES
DILTER
24
RUE ALIBERT
PARIS

BLAIN FILS AINÉ
CULTURES
GRAINES
Saint-Remy-de-Provence

BAZAR de L'HOTEL de VILLE PARIS
Lutter contre les Parasites
FERMES
JARDINS

MAISON SPÉCIALE
L'HORTICULTURE & L'AGRICULTURE
THIOLON
8, QUAI DE LA MÉGISSERIE
ATELIERS DE CONSTRUCTION A PARIS
180 MÉDAILLES
A partir du 15 Avril 1913 : 16, RUE DU LOUVRE

Sutton's
Amateur's Guide
In Horticulture
for 1893.

VICK QUALITY SEEDS GROW
THE BEST CROPS THE EARTH PRODUCES

CATALOGUE
for the Season
of 1899-1900.

SEED
ANNUAL
1915
D. M. FERRY & Co.
SEEDSMEN
DETROIT
MICH.
SPENCERS MIXED

BURPEE'S
SEEDS THAT GROW
Burpee's Best Five
New Vegetables
W. ATLEE BURPEE CO.
Seed Growers
Philadelphia, Pa. Clinton, Iowa

SOW SALZER'S SEEDS
JOHN A. SALZER SEED CO.
LA CROSSE, WIS.
1868-1924

ABOVE Traditional packaging from a Portuguese seed merchant.

RIGHT Major French seed companies, such as Vilmorin and les Grains des Paysans, would send large, colorful posters like this one, c. 1880, to seed merchants to illustrate their products. At the time, most gardeners could not read but could recognize the images.

AUBERGINE
violette longue
CHOU MILAN
petit hâtif d'Ulm
CHOU ROUGE GROS
OGNON BLANC GROS
OGNON ROUGE FONCÉ
LAITUE
romaine blonde maraichère
CAROTTE
rouge demi-longue de Chantenay
MACHE A GROSSE GRAINE
NAVET RAVE
d'Auvergne hâtif
CHICORÉE SCAROLE
en cornet
CAROTTE
rouge demi-longue Nantaise
MACHE
d'Italie ou Régence
CHOU NAVET BLANC
CAROTTE
rouge demi-courte de Guérande
PISSENLIT ORDINAIRE
(dent-de-lion)
COURGE A LA MŒLLE
USTRÉS
EN COULEUR
RADIS
demi-long violet à bout blanc
CIBOULE COMMUNE
RADIS DEMI LONG
ROSE
CARDON
de Tours
CARDON
plein inerme
RADIS
rond violet à bout blanc
CELERI
plein blanc
RADIS
rond noir d'hiver
CONCOMBRE VERT LONG
CRESSON DE JARDIN
vivace
PIMENT ROUGE
long
CHOU NAVET RUTABAGA
CHAMPION à collet rouge
RADIS
demi-long écarlate à bout blanc
COURGE SUCRIÈRE
du Brésil
RADIS
rond rose à bout blanc
LAITUE
brune d'hiver
NAVET DEMI-LONG
des Vertus race Marteau
blanc
PIMENT
gros carré doux
ÉPINARD
monstrueux de Viroflay
ASPERGE
violette d'Argenteuil
ÉPINARD
à feuille de laitue
TOMATE
rouge grosse hâtive
CHOU-FLEUR GÉANT
d'Automne
SALSIFIS BLANC
TOMATE
rouge naine hâtive
Chromolith. J. L. GOFFART, S.A., Bruxelles

French artist Gustave Caillebotte's painting *The Gardeners*, 1875–77, represents a typical bourgeois nineteenth-century enclosed vegetable garden with its flower bed border and espaliered fruit trees along the south-facing wall. In the traditional manner, the two gardeners are barefoot. Because their feet were always in contact with water, leather or wooden shoes would have disintegrated very quickly. In the rear glass hotbeds protect young plants. The glass cloches, or bell jars, are propped up with small terra-cotta pots for ventilation. The shape of the watering cans is characteristic of those used by vegetable gardeners. Private collection.

An anonymous English photograph, c. 1900, shows two gardeners carting off leaves in a wheelbarrow. They are members of the large staff that maintained the park on a private estate.

BEARBEITUNG DES BODENS

Den eigenen Besitz abzustecken ist wichtig, seitdem die Menschen begonnen haben, bestimmte Stücke Land für sich in Anspruch zu nehmen. Einwanderer oder bereits ansässige Farmer, die sich von ihren Nachbarn abgrenzen wollten, mußten ihr Land genau vermessen und mit Hecken, Mauern oder Grenzsteinen markieren. Sie zu verschieben galt seit jeher als Verbrechen.

Zuerst vermaß man das Land durch Abschreiten. Obwohl dieses Verfahren ungenau ist, liefert es doch angenäherte Werte. Die ersten Marken waren Steine und Pfähle. Man verwendete sie zum Pflanzen von Bäumen und markierte mit ihnen auch den Ort künftiger Anlagen. Im fünfzehnten Jahrhundert war eine dünne Schnur das leichteste und einfachste Gerät zur Längenmessung. Später brachte man in regelmäßigen Abständen Knoten an. Im sechzehnten Jahrhundert waren die Grobschmiede imstande, Drahtstücke mit identischer Länge herzustellen. Man verband sie mit Metallringen und konnte auf diese Weise genauere Messungen durchführen. In Europa wurde das Vermessen so wichtig, daß der französische König Heinrich II. 1554 den Landvermesser als Beruf anerkannte. Zu jener Zeit hatte noch jedes Land seine eigenen Längen- und Flächenmaße, zum Beispiel Daumen, Fuß, Elle, Yard, Morgen, Tagwerk oder Acre.

LINKS Auf dieser französischen Illustration aus dem neunzehnten Jahrhundert gräbt ein Gärtner in Holzschuhen den Boden um, um ihn für die Aussaat vorzubereiten. Im Hintergrund überwacht der Herr mit einem Buch in der Hand die Arbeiten.

Der typische Garten des Mittelalters war klein und von einer Mauer umgeben. Doch während der Renaissance und besonders unter Ludwig XIV. entwickelte sich eine Vorliebe für ausgedehnte geometrische Gärten mit langen Perspektiven, Baumalleen, symmetrisch angelegten Blumenbeeten, mit Wasserbecken und Springbrunnen. Das erforderte genaue Messungen auch von Abhängen und Höhenunterschieden.

Der Kompaß war das wichtigste Instrument, um die Ausrichtung des Gartens festzulegen. Mit Senkschnur, Nivellier- und Wasserwaage legte man die Vertikale und die Horizontale für den Bau von Terrassen und Wegen fest. Diese Geräte waren einfach anzuwenden und blieben jahrhundertelang dieselben. Mit komplizierteren Meßgeräten, die oft aus Instrumenten zur Navigation hervorgegangen waren, bestimmte man Winkel und Höhenunterschiede.

Lag der Gesamtplan eines Gartens fest, so richtete der Gärtner seine Aufmerksamkeit nun auf die Natur und die Tiefe des Bodens. Zuerst wurde er mit Spaten oder Pflug umgebrochen. Kinder entfernten Steine und Wurzeln, die die Gartengeräte ruinieren oder das Wachstum der Pflanzen behindern konnten.

Der Spaten bestand anfänglich ganz aus Holz, wurde später aber mit Metall verstärkt. Das Gerät mit dem Metallblatt und dem Holzgriff veränderte sich kaum im Lauf der Jahrhunderte. Pickel, Gabel und Hacke vervollständigten die Grundausrüstung für die Bodenbearbeitung. Mit einer Harke aus Holz oder Metall glättete man schließlich die Bodenoberfläche.

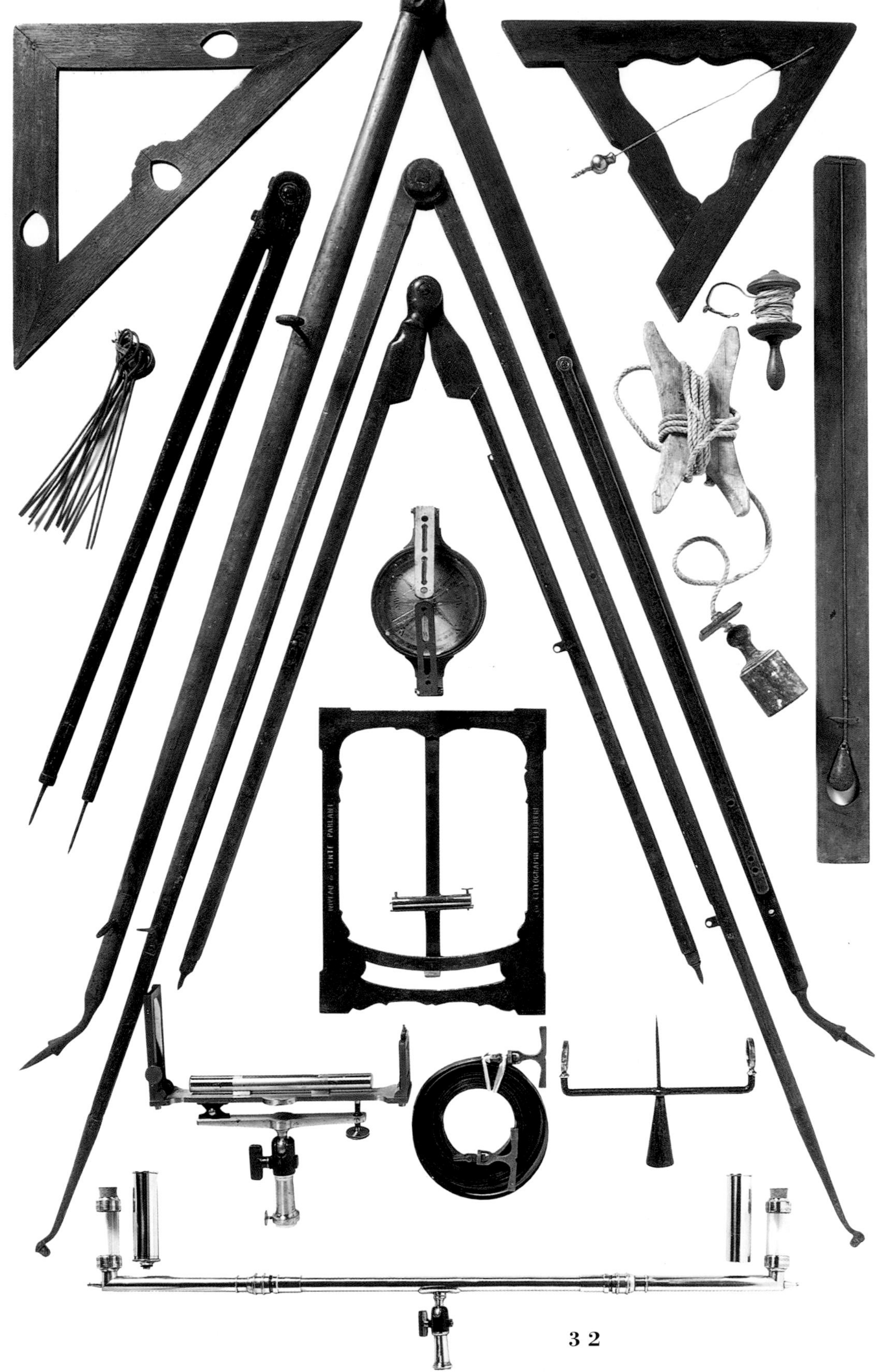

PRECEDING PAGES Under the branches of a hundred-year-old tree in a Normandy garden, the basic tools for staking out, measuring, or redesigning the garden have been laid out. Included are two compasses, a plumb line, a water gauge, and a graduated folding perch.

LEFT AND RIGHT An array of late-eighteenth- and nineteenth-century measuring and planning tools, including siting instruments, compasses, and levelers, that were used to establish the general plan of the garden as well as its different levels, slopes, pathways, and planting sites.

BREVET D'INVENTION
RELIURE — ENTOILAGE
CONCESSION
PERMIS D'EXPLOITATION

Spades come in a variety of shapes for different functions: turning over the soil, digging ditches, planting trees, finishing off the borders of paths and alleys, and cutting peat moss or sod. There are also spades with curved heads for shoveling grain or putting apples and potatoes into sacks. The heads of some spades are designed with openings to lessen their weight and drain water. Handles ending in a Y or T shape, which makes the work easier, have been around since Roman times.

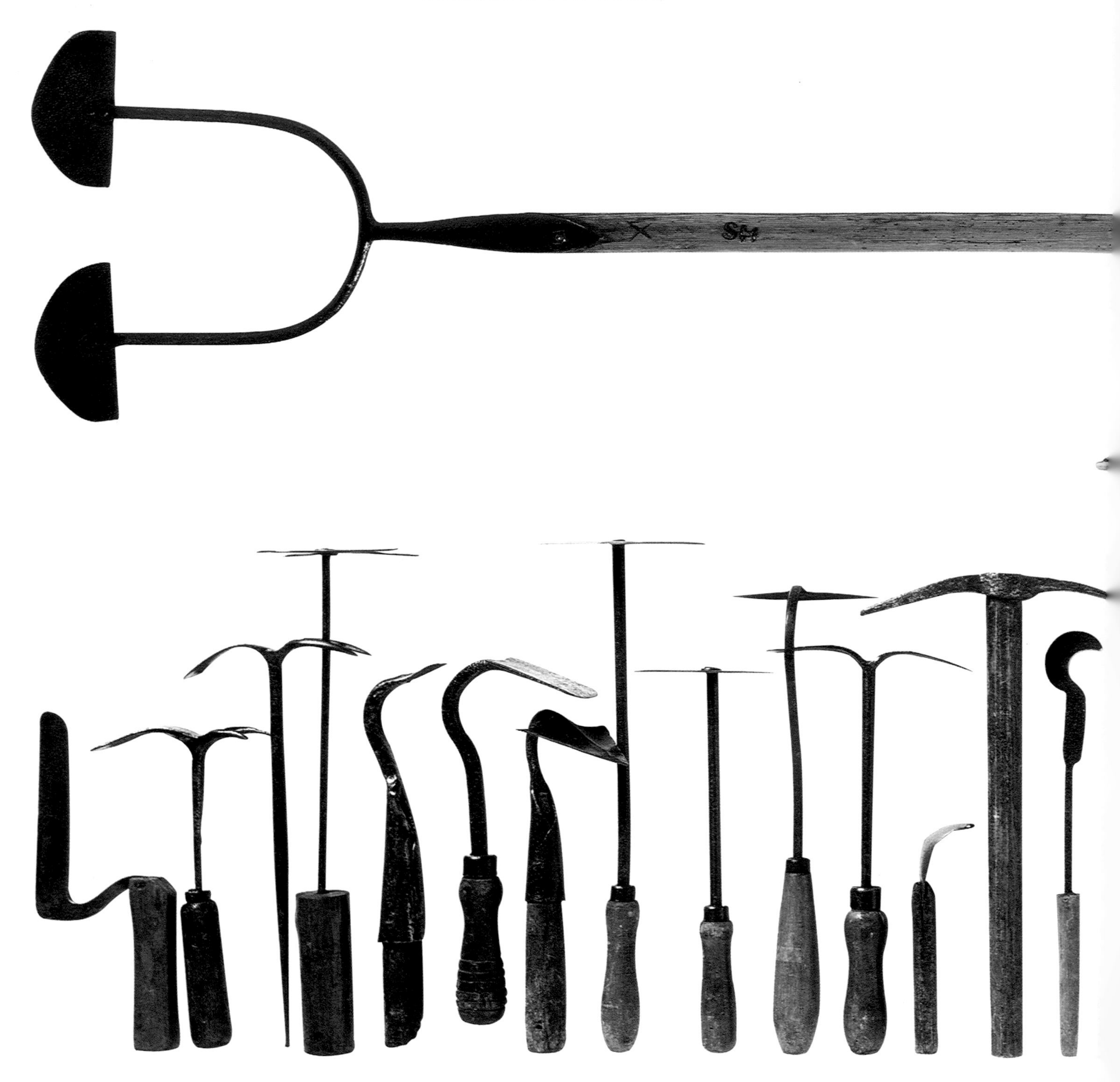

Forks and hoes come in two basic sizes: big for large-scale plantings and small for more precise tasks, such as weeding flower beds and vegetable gardens, transplanting young plants, or maintaining plants in greenhouses and nurseries. The oversize double hoe, top, allowed

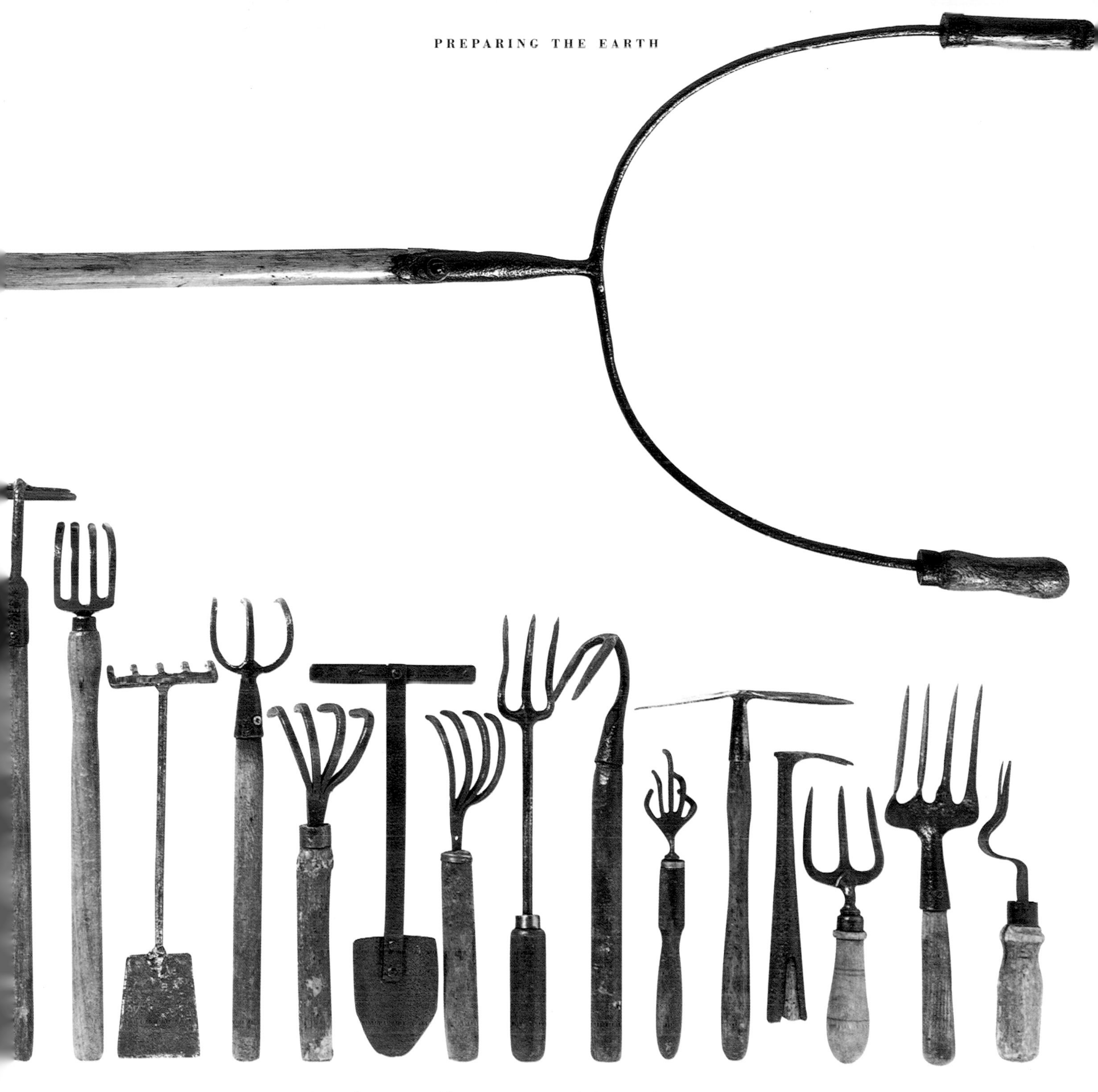

the gardener to weed between two rows of plants at the same time. The smaller variety, bottom, includes, from left, a potato digger, weeding hoes, onion hoes, moss scrapers, claws, garden forks, and a daisy grubber.

LEFT Hand-forged iron forks, sometimes called spade forks, are for pulling out roots or harvesting vegetables such as beets. The horizontal wood or iron elements at the top of the fork heads support the pressure of the gardener's foot.

RIGHT Tools for the preparation of the soil, including a spade with a double-toothed edge, a wooden spade, and a metal spade, are grouped in a garden shed. The round or oval wicker-and-straw sieves, wire-mesh riddles, and winnowing baskets were used to refine the soil by sifting out stones and gravel.

BELOW Paper warranty labels, such as this French one from the turn of the century, would be glued to the polished wooden handles of industrially manufactured tools as a guarantee of their quality.

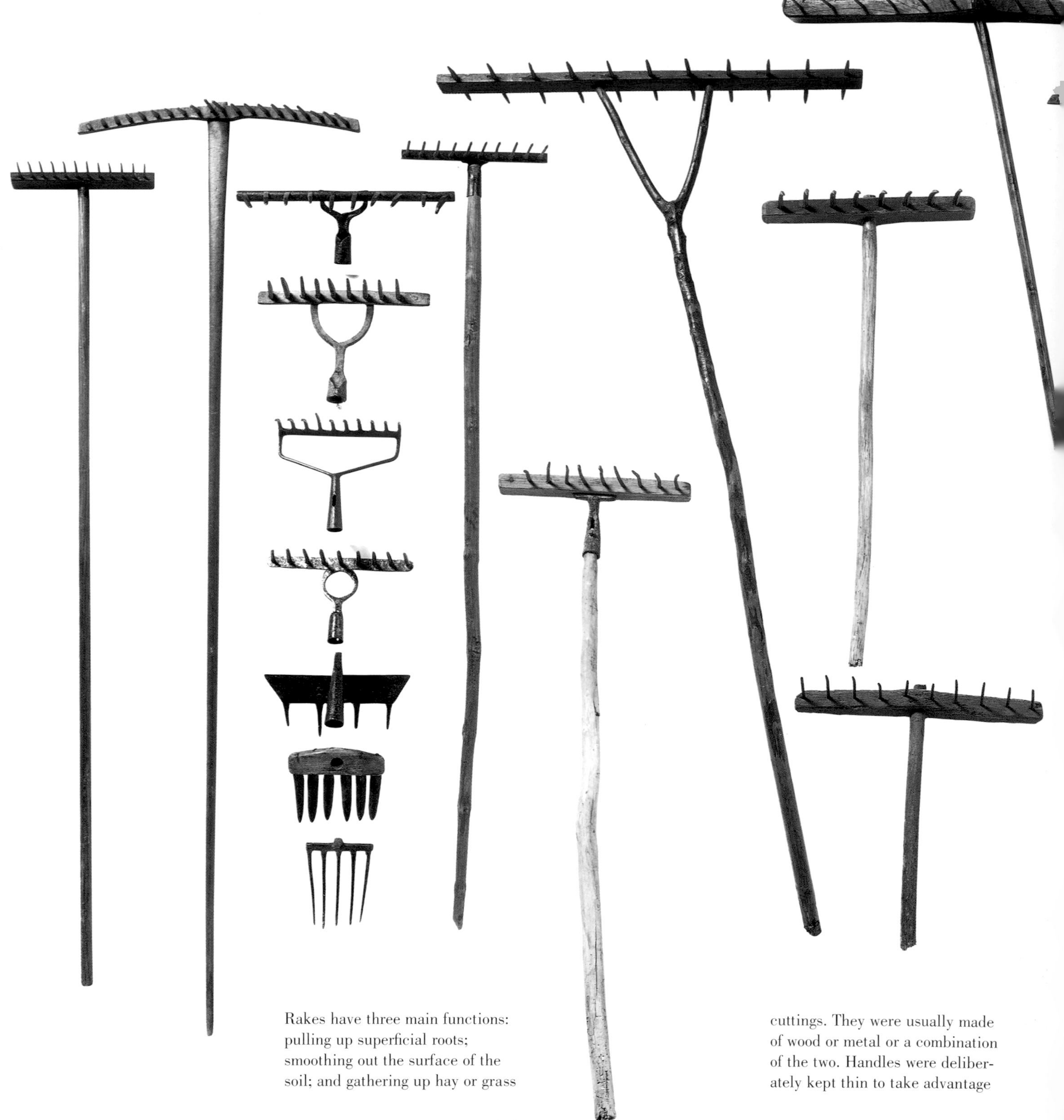

Rakes have three main functions: pulling up superficial roots; smoothing out the surface of the soil; and gathering up hay or grass cuttings. They were usually made of wood or metal or a combination of the two. Handles were deliberately kept thin to take advantage

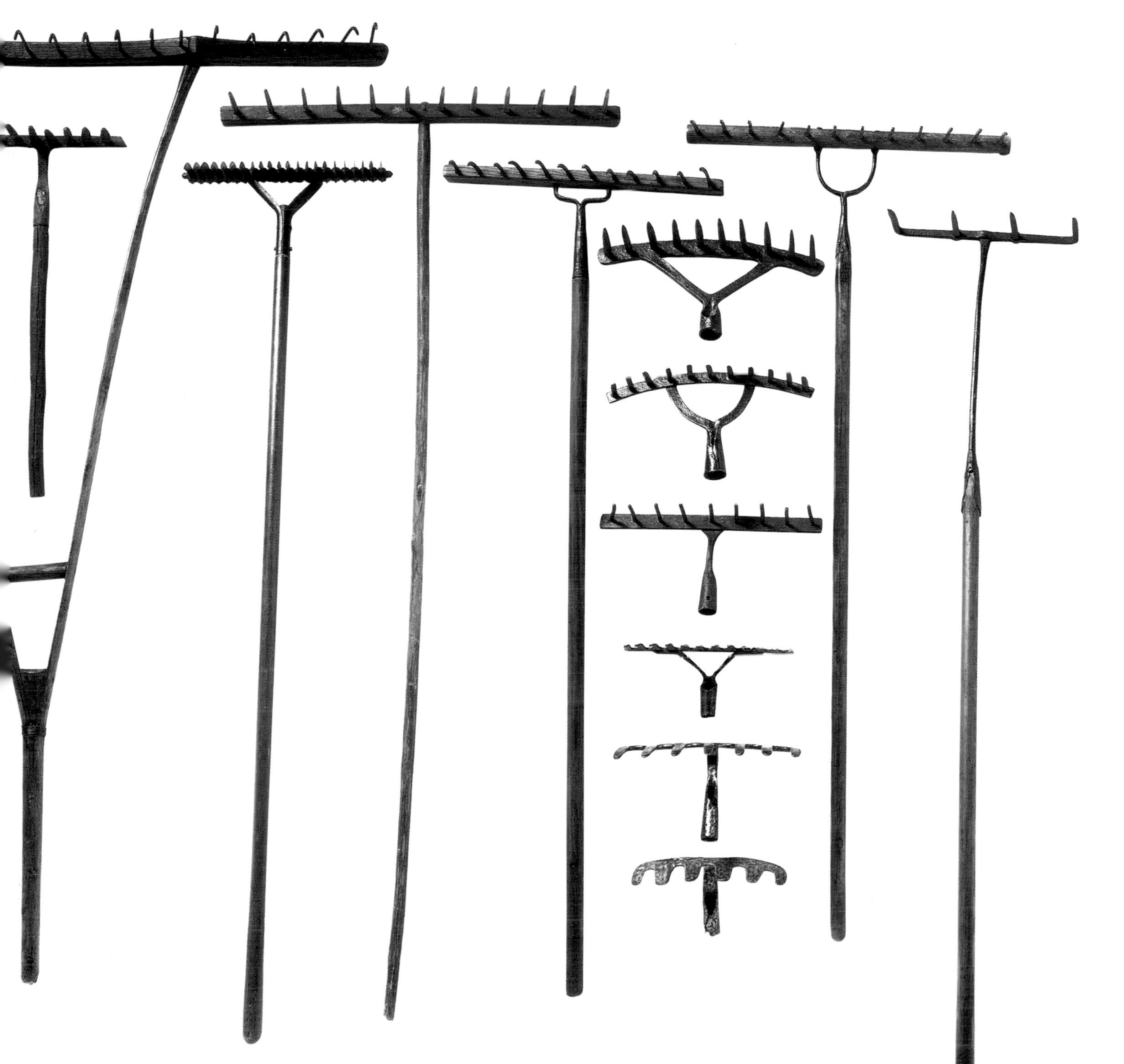

of the flexibility of the wood. Rakes for grass and hay were always made of wood because it was lightweight and easily repaired, whereas rakes for gravel or stones tended to have metal heads reinforced with Y-shaped elements.

L'ÉLITÉINE
l'engrais du vieux jardinier
Laboratoires L. Clause _ Bretigny s/. Orge
ÉLITÉINE
LES IMPR. H.M. BOUTYN. PARIS.

SOWING AND PLANTING

In comparison to the great forces of nature—lightning storms, crashing waves, high winds, bright sun—the act of sowing a seed into a shallow depression in the earth seems almost inconsequential. Yet from the moment that early man discovered that a single grain placed in the ground could generate new growth, the course of human life was changed forever. Awaiting the fruits of what he had sown transformed the once-nomadic hunter and scavenger into a sedentary cultivator.

Every year, as soon as the cold of winter released its grip on the earth, the soil would be prepared for sowing seeds and planting bulbs, tubers, rhizomes or rootstocks, and young plants. Reels of string, dibbers, garden trowels, and seeders were the necessary tools. Seeds were either sown directly into the ground along furrows or placed in cold frames, pots, or greenhouses to sprout before being transplanted into the soil.

The dibber was the tool used to make the hole that received the young plant. The earliest handcrafted examples were made from a piece of horn or bone or from a simple curved branch carved into a point and hardened by the heat of a fire. By the sixteenth century dibbers were equipped with a hammered tin or copper tip, and by the beginning of the nineteenth century they appeared in a profusion of shapes, with two, three, or more teeth. Longer handles helped to reduce back strain. But the Industrial Revolution and the standardization necessitated by mass production in the second half of the nineteenth century put the brakes on the diversity of dibbers; a hundred years later the catalog published by Truffaut, one of the most important French suppliers of gardening equipment and plants, listed only three models.

Porous and sturdy, terra-cotta pots have existed since antiquity. Depicted on Egyptian bas-reliefs dating back to the reign of Ramses II, they were widely used by the Romans to start off seedlings or as ornaments in the house. The terra-cotta pot's simple shape derived from the drinking goblet, and it was traditionally turned on a wheel by the village potter. The rim strengthened the edge of the pot and allowed for stacking a large number of pots one atop the other. A thicker edge supported and protected the stalks of certain hanging plants, such as strawberries and geraniums. Holes could be made in the sides of the pots to accommodate the roots of orchids, for example. The nineteenth-century fondness for growing indoor plants in conservatories led to the elaborate decoration of clay pots, some of which were enameled in an array of colors and motifs.

Today, however, clay pots with imperfections and patinated surfaces are particularly appreciated. When their simple, classic shapes are covered in soft green moss or spotted with traces of calcium, they have a special and evocative charm.

LEFT An advertisement aimed at seed and fertilizer merchants depicts a bearded gardener who seems about to reveal the secret of his successful garden. The quality of this brand of fertilizer is suggested by its name, Elitéine, or, "for the elite."

ABOVE Three steps in the raising of plants from seed are shown: the preparation of finely sifted soil in an earthenware pan that has been perforated for drainage; the storage of seeds from the preceding year in small metal tins with glass covers and glass tubes; and the sprouting of seedlings in a shallow pan.

RIGHT The gardener's drawer is stocked with an assortment of seeds and grains that were either carefully preserved from the previous year's harvest, bought at the local nursery, or ordered from the catalogs of the numerous garden and seed suppliers that flourished in the second half of the nineteenth century.

ROSE TRÉMIÈRE DOUBLE
GRANDE VARIÉE

LEFT, TOP AND BOTTOM Terracotta pots were usually stacked and stored in greenhouses under tables and counters. Bits of glass and pieces of broken clay would be put at the bottom of the pots for drainage before they were filled with soil. Deeper pots were reserved for long-rooted specimens such as alpine plants. The variety of plants necessitated a great number of pots of different dimensions and diameters.

RIGHT A sampling of clay containers, including round and square shallow terrines, top row; two-to-eight-inch-high pots, with and without rims, second row; half-pots that can be hung flush to the wall, bottom row, center; an unusual drainage pipe, bottom row, second from right; and a hyacinth pot, bottom row, far right.

ABOVE Trowels are used mainly for removing plants from pots and planting them in vegetable or flower beds. The head is often elongated, and the blade is sometimes curved to echo the shape of the pot. Trowels used for exotic plants often have unusual shapes: the one shown second from the left is called a fern fork. Narrow trowels were designed for working in confined areas such as window boxes and rock gardens.

In some cases, ordinary spoons were transformed into small trowels that served mainly for removing weeds from pots. The small trowel at the far right is a weeding tool.

OVERLEAF Three rows of green bean plants intersect a field of young lettuces. The tool in the foreground is a green bean planter. Its pointed metal tip makes the holes, while the articulated handle permits the seeds to be planted one by one at desired intervals.

LEFT Garden reels were used not only to help plant straight rows but also to even out the edges of borders and paths. The simplest ones were made by hand out of two sharpened pieces of wood and an ordinary ball of string. While some reels were forged by the local blacksmith, others were manufactured in small factories. Displayed without their cord, they make a strong graphic statement.

RIGHT A selection of dibbers—from the most basic, made of a simple branch, to the most sophisticated, crafted of elm and copper—is assembled on a gardener's worktable. The miniature dibber on the far right was reserved for thinning out young lettuces.

Dibbers—pencil-shaped tools for making planting holes—were usually made by the gardener himself out of branches of various diameters, depending on the sizes of the holes he needed. Some dibbers were made from old pipes or the salvageable handles of broken tools or by recycling bits of metal.

ABOVE With its turned-wood handle and metal funnel, this dibber was used for planting bulbs and potatoes.

RIGHT Round or rectangular shallow boxes with perforated trays served to gauge the size of bulbs and onions.

NURTURING AND PROTECTING

The desire to grow plants regardless of climate or season, to start young seedlings, or to keep alive botanical specimens brought home by explorers and travelers led gardeners to create shelters that could simulate the specific climatic conditions required by the individual plants.

Before the Middle Ages, temporary covers to protect young or fragile plants from wind, rain, and cold were inspired by the primitive shelters that nomads crafted out of branches, straw, and herbs. In the fifteenth and sixteenth centuries cloches, or bell jars, were opaque. Made of rye grass or willow, they were shaped like truncated cones or beehives. Wood-framed shelters in truncated pyramid forms appeared at about the same time. It wasn't until the beginning of the seventeenth century that small, movable greenhouses with lead, copper, iron, and later, cast-iron frames supporting small panes of glass were developed. The glass replaced the mica or oiled paper that had been in use since the Romans practiced forcing plants in wood-framed containers. Those containers are the ancestors of the cold frames that can still be found in most gardens today.

Bell-shaped glass cloches are first mentioned in gardening treatises about 1630. They continued to be made for three centuries, especially in small factories in eastern France. Glass blowers would make the twenty-five-inch-wide by twenty-five-inch-high cloches both with and without glass knobs. By the nineteenth century some vegetable gardeners had as many as ten thousand cloches in a variety of shapes and sizes. But the European factories disappeared during the bombardments of World War I, and by 1916 new production had ceased. Nevertheless, the popularity of glass cloches did not diminish until the 1940s, when they were gradually replaced by plastic tunnels. Today glass and terra-cotta cloches are more often used as decorative elements in the garden or house than for their original purpose.

In the ruins at Pompeii there are remains of rooms for sheltering plants during the cold months. At the end of the seventeenth century orangeries and *citronières*—special rooms for orange, lemon, and palm trees and other delicate plants—were in fashion, modeled after the enormous orangery built for Louis XIV in 1685 at Versailles to shelter more than 1,200 exotic trees. The first structure resembling the greenhouses of today was built in 1680 for the duke of Devonshire at Chatsworth in the north of England. But it was only in the nineteenth century that technological advances made monumental greenhouses, such as the Crystal Palace, built by Sir Joseph Paxton in 1851, possible. Their popularity created a rage for individual greenhouses, and soon fanciful glass-and-metal structures, transformed into plant-filled winter gardens and conservatories, became a natural addition to nearly every Victorian house.

LEFT Jane Maria Bowkett's painting *A Young Lady in a Conservatory*, c. 1870, illustrates the Victorian penchant for indoor gardens. Roy Miles Gallery/The Bridgeman Art Library.

PRECEDING PAGES From the seventeenth century on, bell-shaped glass cloches were handblown in large quantities, especially for the gardeners who provided fresh vegetables to the expanding towns. Although hundreds of thousands were made, no two are identical in color and size. Each has its own imperfections—bubbles trapped in the glass and surface irregularities that give it a distinct personality. The varied coloration of the glass—cloudy white, pale pink, blue, or green—is a function of the varying chemical composition of the sand used in its fabrication. Modern, machine-made reproduction cloches are produced primarily in Italian and eastern European glass factories; they are thicker and do not possess the finesse and lightness of their handcrafted ancestors.

RIGHT A rare glazed terra-cotta cloche, made in the Loire Valley by a potter and used for blanching lettuce.

LEFT Handmade late-nineteenth-century terra-cotta cloches have ventilation holes to prevent spoilage from excessive heat or humidity. This type of cloche was usually used to blanch lettuces and slow their growth.

BELOW An unusual six-inch-high nineteenth-century glass cloche from Holland, designed especially for hyacinths.

RIGHT Terra-cotta cloches similar in shape to chimney pots were for forcing rhubarb. Measuring about twenty inches in diameter and thirty inches in height, they were sometimes equipped with lids of the same material.

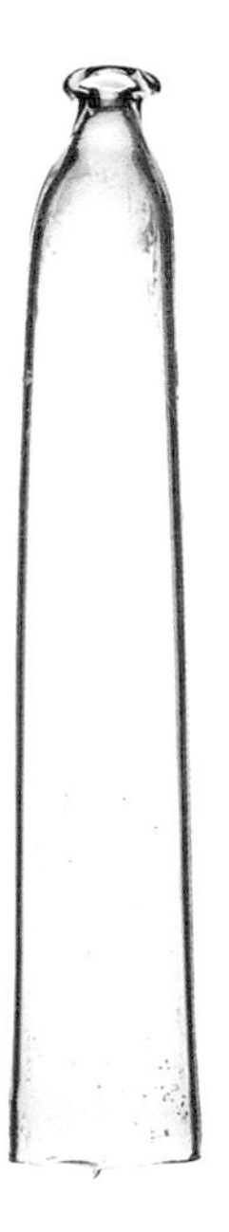

LEFT An elongated glass cloche made specifically for growing a single cucumber. The hole in the top is just wide enough for the stalk of the plant to be inserted and for air to circulate.

BELOW The truncated-pyramid type of cloche for sheltering young lettuces was popular because it was easily made from thin wood boards.

RIGHT Metal-framed glass cloches date from the eighteenth and nineteenth centuries. Whiting the panes was sometimes necessary to shade plants from direct sunlight. One of the panes was always removable for ventilation, and putty or ceruse, a white lead pigment, was used to repair cracks in the glass. Shaped like small architectural tents or pavilions, these cloches now usually serve a decorative function.

OVERLEAF The rounded greenhouse that sits in the center of a flower garden outside Paris is typical of those that made their appearance at the beginning of the eighteenth century. The curved shape maximized the hours of sunlight the plants received.

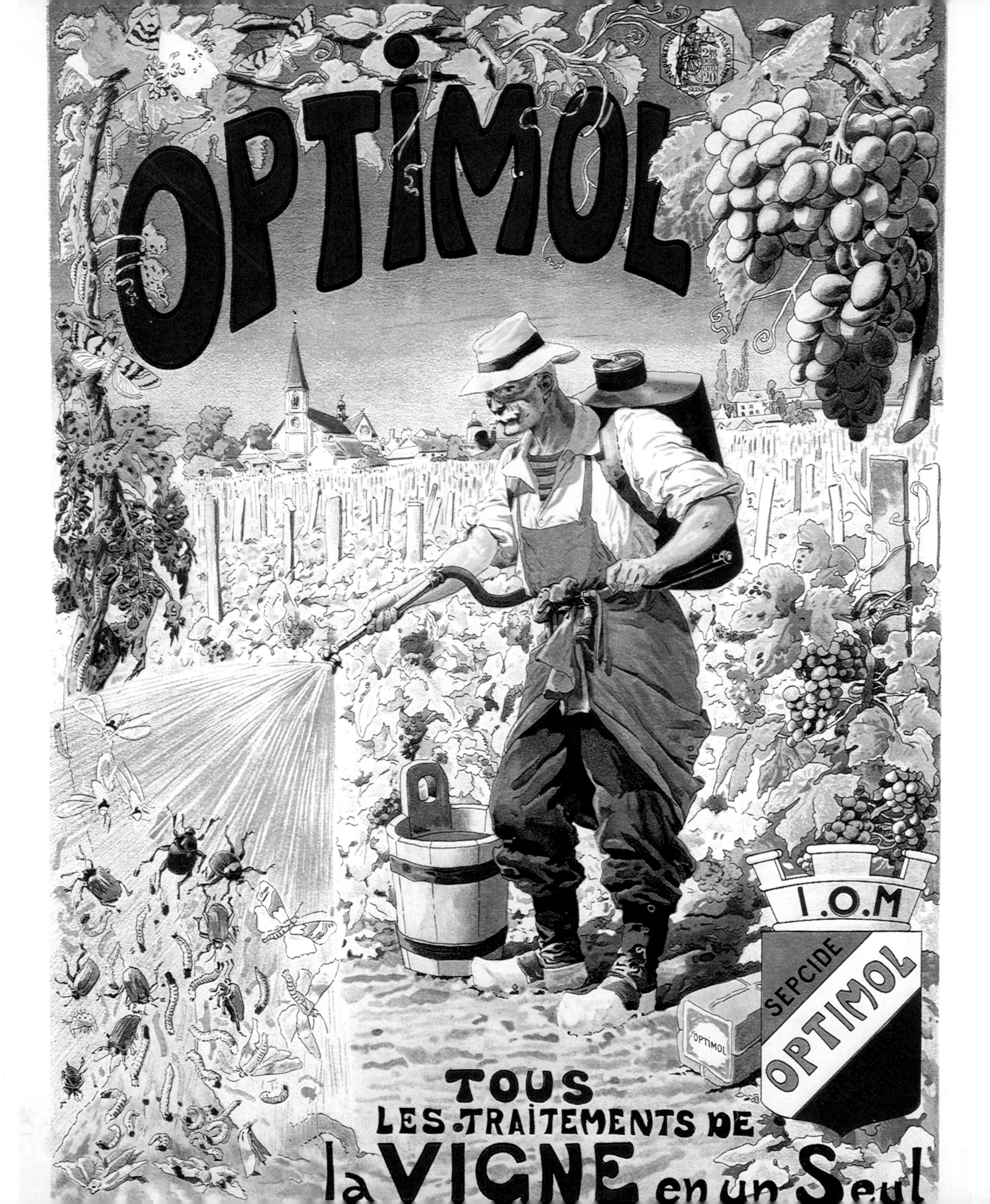
OPTIMOL
I.O.M
SEPCIDE
OPTIMOL
OPTIMOL
TOUS
LES TRAITEMENTS DE
la VIGNE en un Seul

DEALING WITH PESTS

One of the most important and least expensive ways to renew the garden was—and still is—to preserve seeds, pips, and stones for planting the following year. In the seventeenth and eighteenth centuries, when farms and gardens had to be self-sufficient, in part because the commercial sale of seeds was not yet widespread, the seeds would be harvested at just the right moment and then dried carefully so they could be stored for the following year without rotting.

The fight against such predators as mice, rats, and voles, as well as bacteria, mildew, fungi, and flying or crawling insects was another major concern for the gardener. Before chemicals were introduced to control garden pests, empirical methods and traditional basic products were the only preventive measures taken to combat the greedy and insatiable predators.

Tree trunks were swabbed with a mixture of sulfur and pitch or ashes and lemon juice; bands of zinc or lead were tied around trees to protect them from hordes of creeping insects; fumigation and the destruction of insect eggs with acid were also widely adopted. Gardeners would burn tobacco leaves to asphyxiate the insects and, using copper syringes, spray infested areas with a concoction of water and macerated tobacco leaves. Until the mid-nineteenth century, iron sulfate and sulfur were the two most frequently used pesticides.

The image of the gardener carrying a large pulverizer or small sprayer on his back was familiar, especially in the vineyards. Without a doubt the most famous fungicide of the late nineteenth century in France was Bouillie Bordelaise, or Bordeaux mixture—copper sulfate and lime—which was dissolved in water and applied to protect vines from mildew. In America at that time, powdered pyrethrum, a kind of chrysanthemum, was often the main ingredient in many commonly used spray insecticides. It was packaged and sold in the general store as Powder of Persia or Persian Insect Powder. Arsenic-based products were also applied to plants to deter pests.

To resist acid corrosion, insecticide pulverizers had to be made of copper. Left unused, their oxidized surface takes on a green patina. But to regain their luster, all these copper beauties need is a spot of polish and a bit of elbow grease. Today plastic has replaced the old copper utensils.

Hunting techniques were adapted to catch undesirable visitors to the garden, and snares, traps, nets, nooses, and glue became the gardener's accomplices. To protect fruit from caterpillars, slugs, mealybugs, birds, or wasps, gardeners would tie thin glazed and translucent paper bags around the stems. Gauze bags, tied around the fruit with string once it reached the size of a walnut, could preserve its unblemished skin.

LEFT A French advertising poster of the 1870s for a well-known brand of pesticide was both eye-catching and easy to understand when it was displayed in the windows of the general store. The gardener, with his clogs, straw hat, and ample blue apron, carries a fifteen-liter reservoir on his back. The attacked insects have been intentionally exaggerated.

ECLIP
MODE D'E

PRECEDING PAGES Displayed on a garden table are two kinds of sprayers: the portable one in the foreground was used to treat plants in flower beds, greenhouses, and conservatories. The larger and more powerful one was cumbersome, but its long hose could reach high branches, alleviating the need for a ladder.

LEFT These mid-nineteenth-century powder-filled bellows for attacking aphids resemble those that were used for powdering wigs and gloves.

RIGHT Copper sulfate and a tin of Bordeaux mixture were two essential weapons in the French gardener's arsenal against pests. The two glass bottles are topped with vaporizer tubes, which allowed for a more accurate gauging of insecticide dosages. The copper syringe attached to a copper reservoir was a time-saving innovation dating from the early nineteenth century.

Bouillie
Nouvelle
SEMEUSE
unique
LA VIGNE
Notre Bouillie
spécial,
Viticulteurs
qui veulent faire à
un traitement
et les préserver
du Mildew

ABOVE Pulverizers enabled copper sulfate or sulfur powders to be sprayed without water. Collectors today appreciate the colorful graphics and striking lettering, which have not faded with time.

RIGHT In a greenhouse filled with young vines, a long-necked pulverizer hangs next to a grape-cutting knife. Thanks to such pulverizers, even the most hard-to-reach grapes grow to maturity.

A metal bucket with a hand pump and a filter was an alternative to the heavier sprayer that was carried on the gardener's back. Its supple rubber hose, capped with a metal vaporizer head, was easy to operate. The apple and pear trees receive a dose of diluted pesticide several times a year.

LEFT A niche in a garden wall is home to wire cages and traps. The rat poison in the large round can is wheat impregnated with arsenic.

RIGHT, TOP Gauze bags keep flying insects away from young pears.

RIGHT, BOTTOM A glass fly trap hangs off the branch of an apple tree. Filled with sugar water, it attracts flies and wasps. Once inside the bottle, insects cannot escape.

LOTERIE NATIONALE

11E TRANCHE 1942

TIRAGE LE 30 JUILLET

WATERING

Water has always been the symbol of life, and to gardeners it is also the very "soul of vegetation," as Jean de La Quintinye, Louis XIV's head gardener, once said. For centuries gardeners have sought solutions to the problems of supplying water to, and storing it in the vicinity of, their plants. The fear of dry spells and drought is a constant even in the more temperate climates.

Although rain is the best source of water, its unreliability has driven gardeners to develop different ways of controlling the flow of water to plants. Cisterns, metal vats, even simple wooden tubs—once the main storage receptacles for water—were placed at different points in the garden to facilitate distribution. And gravity, an endless and free source of power, was employed wherever possible to keep water flowing.

Since the days of the Sumerians and the Romans, gardeners have been thinking up new devices to move and distribute water, perfecting hydraulic machines, windmills, hand pumps, and later, steam and electric pumps. But it was the appearance, about 1830, of a system of articulated metal pipes mounted on wheels, as well as the production of rubber pipes at the turn of the century, that greatly expanded the possibilities of watering.

The watering can is a basic garden tool. Originally water was carried in goatskin or leather pouches, then in terra-cotta containers that served both the kitchen and the garden. Called first vases, then vessels, the containers became known as watering cans only about the mid-eighteenth century. The modest cost of terra-cotta popularized the fragile containers, the one inconvenience of which was their weight.

The first iron watering cans were more durable than their terra-cotta counterparts, but their round shape made them difficult to manage. Indeed, the watering can kept its round shape for centuries, until the end of the seventeenth century, when it took on the shape we now recognize. And it was not until about 1750 that the flow of water from these receptacles could be regulated to suit more delicate flowers or hardier rows of vegetables.

In the eighteenth century most of the better watering cans were made of copper. They resisted corrosion well, and when no longer in use, they could be sold for the price of the metal itself. But by the end of the nineteenth century, as the cost of copper rose, most watering cans were made of zinc, iron, or galvanized tin.

In spite of the invasion of plastics in the 1950s, old-fashioned metal watering cans remain the favorites of many gardeners. To prolong their life, they should be turned upside down to dry after use. They should also be fitted with a rose (perforated cap or plate) and filled with water that has been kept at an ambient temperature—which explains the presence and usefulness of basins in vegetable gardens. Watering in full sun should be avoided because the droplets of water concentrate the sun's rays and burn plants' leaves.

LEFT This French poster was commissioned during World War II to encourage the cultivation of family gardens. The idealized image of the gardener, with his athletic build, perfectly cut pants, and immaculate shirt, was in striking contrast to the harsh reality of wartime.

LEFT A metal rolling water tank, dating from about 1860, could hold up to sixty gallons of water. The long-handled metal pail in front of it was useful for getting water from deep or otherwise inaccessible sources.

ABOVE An early twentieth-century watering device that gently moistened new seedbeds. On hot summer days it was also used to keep the dust from rising along garden paths.

ABOVE Frog- and turtle-shaped cast-iron sprinklers equipped with copper piping were made in limited quantities at the end of the nineteenth century for watering lawns or decorating basins.

ABOVE A French mobile watering system includes an elaborate rotating sprinkler. The water pressure activates a crenellated wheel, which rotates the water 360 degrees.

RIGHT The wooden hose holder on wheels became indispensable in France from the moment it was first widely produced, about 1860. Easy to use and inexpensive, it enabled heavy rubber hoses to be moved without damaging paths or plants.

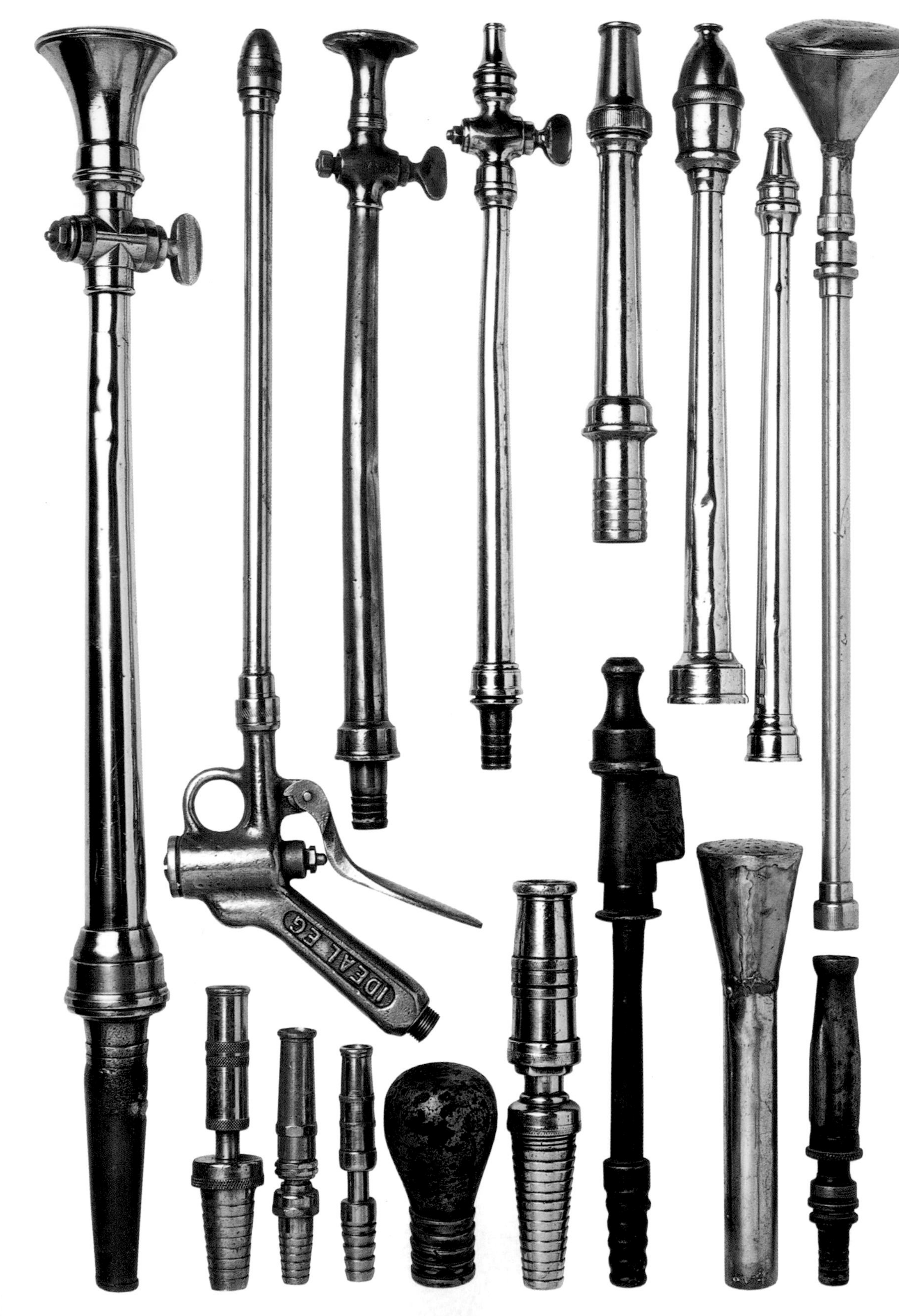

LEFT Sprayers, with and without caps, were made in varying lengths and widths, depending on the water pressure and desired intensity of spray.

RIGHT Sprayers with fan-shaped ends provided a wide-angled jet of water. Although mass-produced for the most part, some were specially crafted from recycled elements, such as the ends of gas lamps.

An early-nineteenth-century professional vegetable gardener's iron watering can features a mobile metal handle. Its characteristic squat shape is reinforced at the waist and base. It can hold up to three gallons of water.

A classical eighteenth-century copper watering can with a double handle could be filled quickly because the straight part of the handle allowed it to be easily submerged in a basin. The shape also made for more rapid watering.

A selection of iron and galvanized-steel watering cans, dating from the mid-nineteenth century—those equipped with large, fixed roses—and the mid-twentieth century—the more streamlined models with adjustable roses.

There are as many shapes of watering cans as there are days in the year. The best ones were made of copper to resist rust and corrosion, but the majority were iron. Early shapes (center row, first four from left) were inspired by the containers that were used to carry water into the kitchen. Some had long spouts for watering hard-to-reach plants in greenhouses. The one with a beak and an especially long nose (bottom

row, second from right) could reach the middle of the flower beds. The unusually shaped watering can at far left, bottom row, was designed to be held by an articulated support on top of a long pole and maneuvered by a rope to water hanging plants or the tops of tree ferns.

LEFT Old terra-cotta watering vessels, sometimes glazed in green or brown, are extremely hard to find in good condition. In the sixteenth and seventeenth centuries they were made to order by local potters, but few have survived the ravages of time.

RIGHT Typical late-nineteenth-century zinc and iron watering cans. The round handles were made in various sizes to accommodate the different sizes of gardeners' hands.

FLEURANCE
ANGERS

COUTELLERIE
FLEURANCE
LA PLUS ANCIENNE DE LA RÉGION · FONDÉE IL Y A DEUX SIÈCLES
Fabrique de SÉCATEURS
7, rue des Pöeliers ANGERS PRÈS DE LA RUE DU MAIL

PRUNING

Removing branches, carving pieces of wood, nipping fruit by the stem, pruning trees, dividing roots, and training young trees are just some of the ordinary tasks the gardener performs all year round. Hunting weapons were the antecedents of the sharp tools the gardener always carried with him for these purposes. Early on it was discovered that rounded blades not only strengthened the force of the cut but also gripped the branch or stem, resulting in a speedier, more precise cut.

Among all the knives, grafters, saws, scythes, and small hatchets that were the gardener's allies in cutting and shaping trees and bushes, the billhook, a weapon with a hooked blade, was the gardener's main cutting tool. Its handle, originally made from a piece of raw wood, was eventually curved to fit more smoothly in the hand and ensure a safer grip. Stag horn, ebony, boxwood, and ash were the materials most often used. Folding blades, introduced in the seventeenth century, were an important safety improvement.

In the seventeenth century the grafting of apples, pears, peaches, and plums became very fashionable at the European courts, and head gardeners were held in high esteem for their inventive attempts to develop new varieties of fruit through grafting techniques.

The pruner is a relatively recent invention, created in France by the marquis de Moleville in 1815. Despite its revolutionary cutting method, it took some fifty years before the pruner became the indispensable tool it still is today. In the second half of the nineteenth century knife manufacturers who realized the commercial possibilities of the new invention introduced changeable blades, more finely forged steel, and different spring mechanisms. The result was a mind-boggling array of designs. There were pruners especially scaled for ladies' hands, and pruners for flower cutting, clipping roses, picking grapes, and turning bushes into topiaries. By the end of the nineteenth century pruners were as common in Victorian winter gardens and flower-cutting rooms as in orchards.

At the turn of the century, gardens and gardening were all the rage. Ladies, who were not supposed to get their hands dirty, would occupy themselves with picking flowers and pressing them in ornate scrapbooks or painting still lifes of them. There were delicate pruners designed specifically for these genteel activities. Men, meanwhile, viewed gardens as an indication of social position—the more elaborate the garden, the greater the affirmation of status. Often their tools were custom-made by well-known cutlers, who ornamented them with coats of arms or monograms, and stored in special leather cases. Though hardly ever used, they are masterpieces of their kind.

LEFT A 1940s poster touts the quality and fame of a factory that made only pruners. The cool, sharp precision of the blue steel pruner is strikingly set off by the warm saffron yellow fields.

LEFT Eighteenth- and nineteenth-century specialized cutting tools with parrot-beak heads were screwed or hammered onto the ends of ten-foot-long poles and used to cut out caterpillar nests, remove mistletoe, or lop off branches.

RIGHT An early-twentieth-century multipurpose cutting kit consists of a modular wooden handle with various attachments, including a lopper, a saw, and a pair of scissors for clipping rows of pleached lindens. The attachments screw onto the end of the handle.

LEFT An unusual 1920s tool is a combination saw and pruner. The saw was for cutting large branches; the pruner, for finishing off the task.

RIGHT The thick trunks of fruit trees necessitated long-bladed saws. The curved blade facilitated the work, and the rounded wood handle was easy to grip.

BELOW A saw with a handle whimsically shaped like a human leg, and a rustic turn-of-the-century toolbox with a saw secured by leather ties to the outside.

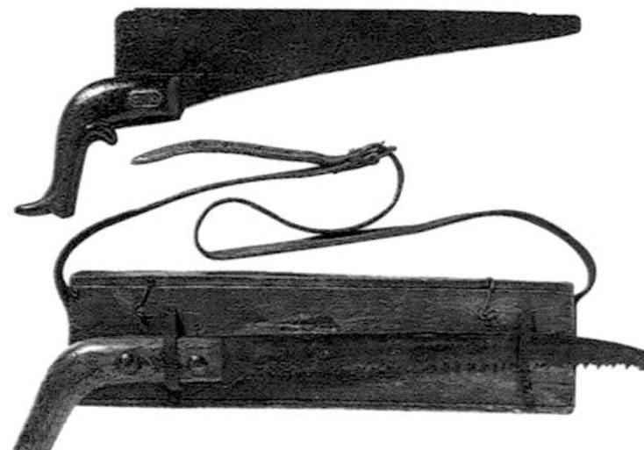

BELOW A German leather tool kit, dated 1940, contains a series of interchangeable blades.

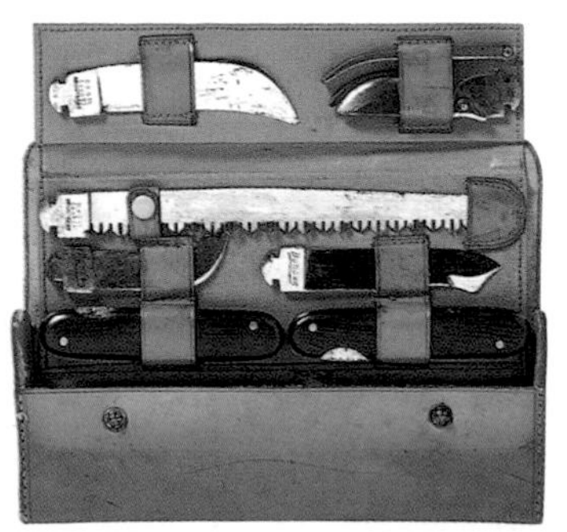

For hundreds of years before the pruner was invented in the early nineteenth century, gardeners relied on billhooks for cutting tasks. The small billhook with the ring at the end of its handle was found in a Roman tomb. The second from the right was discovered in the moat of

a thirteenth-century castle during an archaeological dig. The extra piece of metal attached to the billhook in the center was used as a hatchet by winegrowers. Although handles came in a wide variety of shapes, the easiest and safest to use were those shaped to fit the palm of the hand.

A dozen pruners, each with a different shape and mechanism. The top right one folds into the handle of a pocket knife; the one next to it is for cutting small flowers; a folding pocket scissors, top left, is also a flower pruner. The pruner second from left, bottom row, is equipped with an elaborate mechanism that operates on a vertical axis.

A huge, triple-headed winegrower's tool dating from the late nineteenth century incorporates a hatchet, a billhook, and a pruner.

The tiny pruner is extremely rare, and was probably custom-made for a child.

A parade of pruners includes tools to snip and cut the most delicate of flowers or the thickest of branches. Sometimes pruners were fashioned from the iron of worn-out steel files. Because they had to be sharp at all times, many featured a large screw that could be loosened to access the cutting blade for sharpening. By 1900 higher-gauge steel rendered this operation less important.

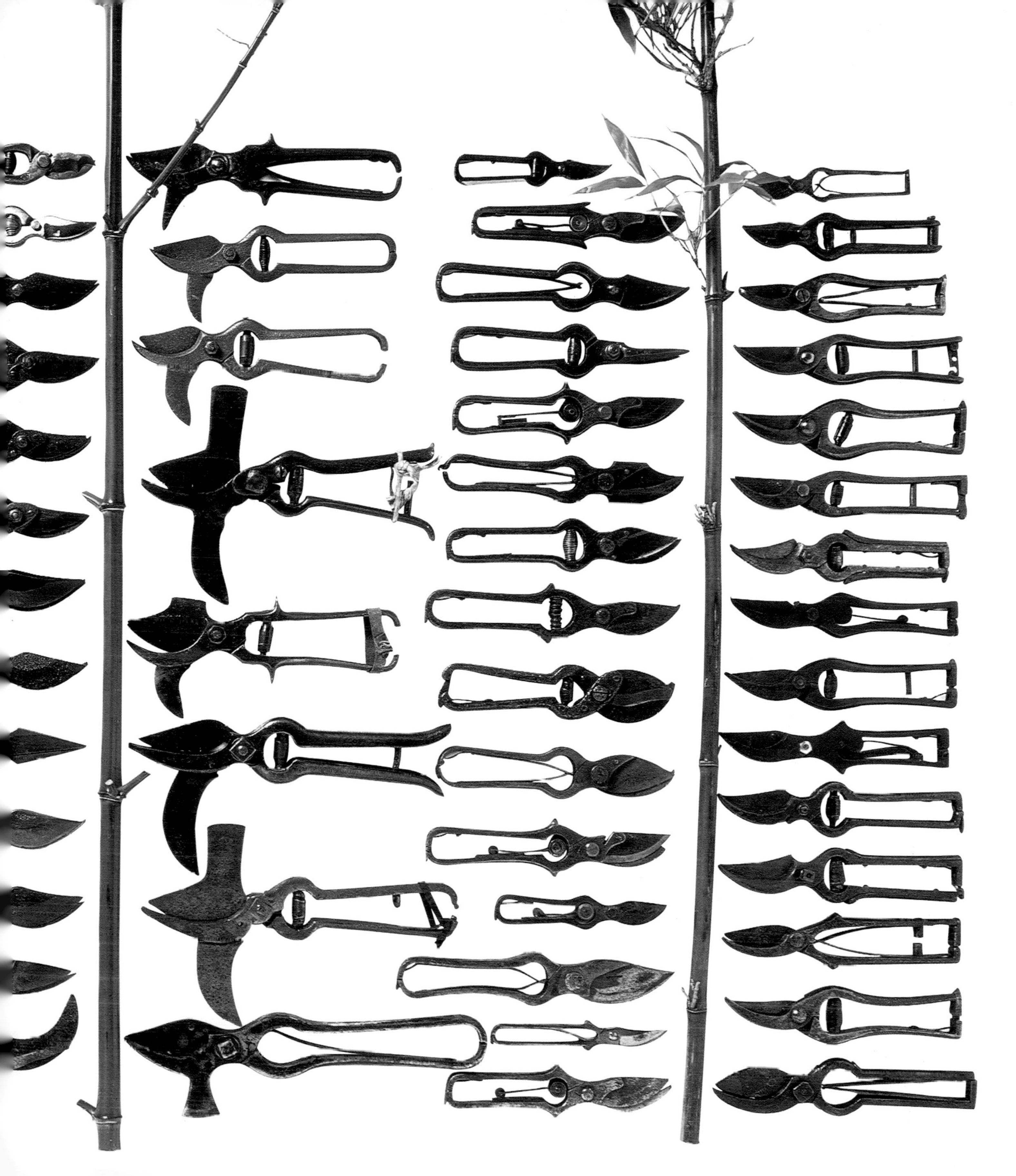

ABOVE A long-handled pruner especially for clipping hard-to-reach climbing roses. A ring in the handle operated the cutting mechanism. The ingenious design, created and patented in France, was exported all over Europe and was particularly popular in England.

BELOW An early-seventeenth-century pruner for cutting roses or the flowers of climbing plants. The work of an arms maker, this rare instrument has the quality and finesse of the weapons of the period, the same close attention to detail: like the hammer of a gun, a string releases the trigger that activates the blade.

RIGHT The blades of sturdy billhooks were often engraved with the initials of the owner, the name of the manufacturer, and an identification number. The handles were made of wood, cow horn, or stag horn.

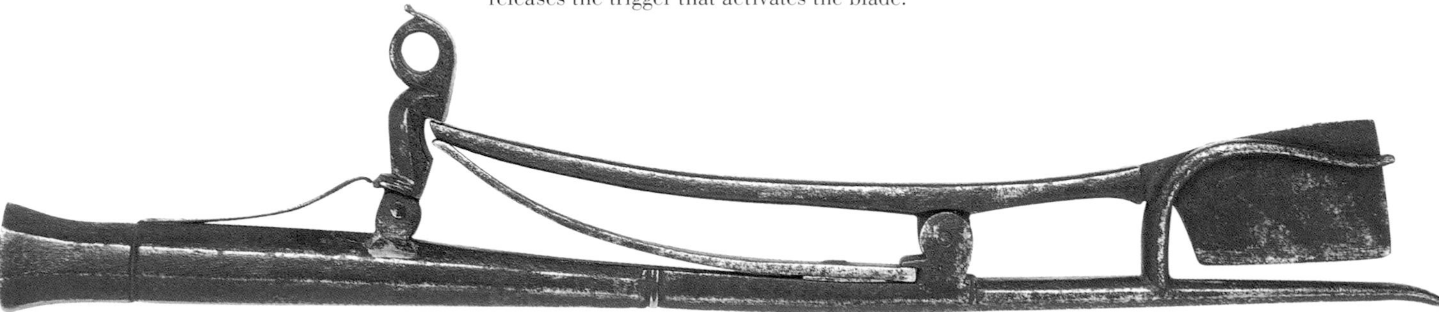

BLANCHARD
PARIS
2

PRUNING

There was a billhook in every gardener's pocket. Though they came in many shapes and materials, most of them had a protruding blade that could be pulled out easily, even with wet or calloused fingers.

Grafting tools are more refined than pruners because the procedure requires great precision and care. The sharp blade was for making the incisions; the tip of the handle, often made of ivory or bone, was for pulling off the branch bark without damaging it.

Pincers were for removing pieces of bark at the grafting spot. Only keen gardeners were successful at grafting. Because grafting was fashionable in the mid-nineteenth century, nursery catalogs of the period were filled with varieties of plants that no longer exist.

VITA
VITA
VITA
Henri Le Monnier
LES GRAINES VIVANTES
VITA
EN VENTE ICI
EN VENTE ICI
VITA VALENCE - R.C. ROMANS 54 B 54
IMP. LE HENAFF St ETIENNE

HARVESTING

Since antiquity, the harvest has been a time of celebration and joy. It was the most eagerly awaited event of the year and the tangible result of the gardener's work. A successful harvest required not only good weather but swift pickers who were attentive and careful. The gardener was also in a race with numerous other enthusiasts of ripe fruits and vegetables, both fur-covered and feathered.

Harvesting the bounty of the garden was carried out by hand for the most part, and great care was taken not to damage or crush fragile vegetables and fruits. The gardener's role included sorting, deciding what should be stored, and overseeing the packing of the merchandise destined for the market or the kitchen in crates and baskets of all shapes and sizes. Most of these baskets were made of willow, oak, chestnut, or hazel. Honeysuckle and bramble, as well as rye grass, straw, rattan, and reeds, could be crafted into lightweight and durable carriers that stood up to everyday use and inclement weather. Whether tied to the gardener's arm, balanced on his head, or hung on his back, baskets were ingeniously molded and adapted to different parts of the body. There were shallow, flat baskets for flowers; baskets with lids for berries; hods that were carried over the shoulder; and wattles made of twigs and branches that served to dry fruits such as plums.

Shaking or beating the tree with a wooden pole was certainly one of the first harvesting methods. And while some vegetables could simply be pulled out of the ground by hand and some fruits picked directly off the tree, many other crops required harvesting tools such as spades, hooks, and hoes. The old reliable multipurpose knife would give birth to more specialized tools such as the potato-picking knife, the asparagus knife, and the dahlia knife.

Ladders allowed the fruit harvester to work more quickly and precisely without hurting either the fruit or the tree. Fruit pickers, which first made their appearance in 1750 and were originally called *pomettes*, or "little apples," were shaped like vases or small baskets and had crenellated edges that caught the stem of the fruit and separated it from the branch. Made of wood, thick wire, or tole, and often ornamented more or less artistically with geometric or floral motifs, fruit pickers were usually tied to the ends of fifteen-foot poles.

Once picked and sorted, fruits were placed on wooden racks, arranged so they didn't touch one another, in dark, cool, well-ventilated rooms that assured their preservation. In this way it was possible for the pleasures of fall to be savored and enjoyed all through the winter.

LEFT The scale of both the jolly gardener and his vegetables is exaggerated in a 1920s French advertising poster, which was displayed in garden shops and seed supply stores.

PRECEDING PAGES Ripe, colorful pumpkins have been carried from the garden in a wooden hand-barrow that dates from the beginning of the century. The tool with the curved blade was used exclusively to weed the spaces between cobblestones.

LEFT Freshly picked plums are piled high in baskets and crates near the entrance to a storehouse. Leaning up against the wall are two chestnut wattles, used for drying the plums in the sun.

RIGHT Baskets for transporting strawberries had specific design features. The corners were reinforced to bear the weight of a number of baskets stacked one on top of the other. The lid was convex so that it would fit snugly into the concave bottom of the basket stacked above it. The gardener marked the baskets with his initials when he consigned them to the wholesaler.

Fruit pickers, whether homemade or manufactured, were often fancifully decorated, underscoring the respect gardeners had for the fruit itself. Those that were homemade were usually crafted of wood

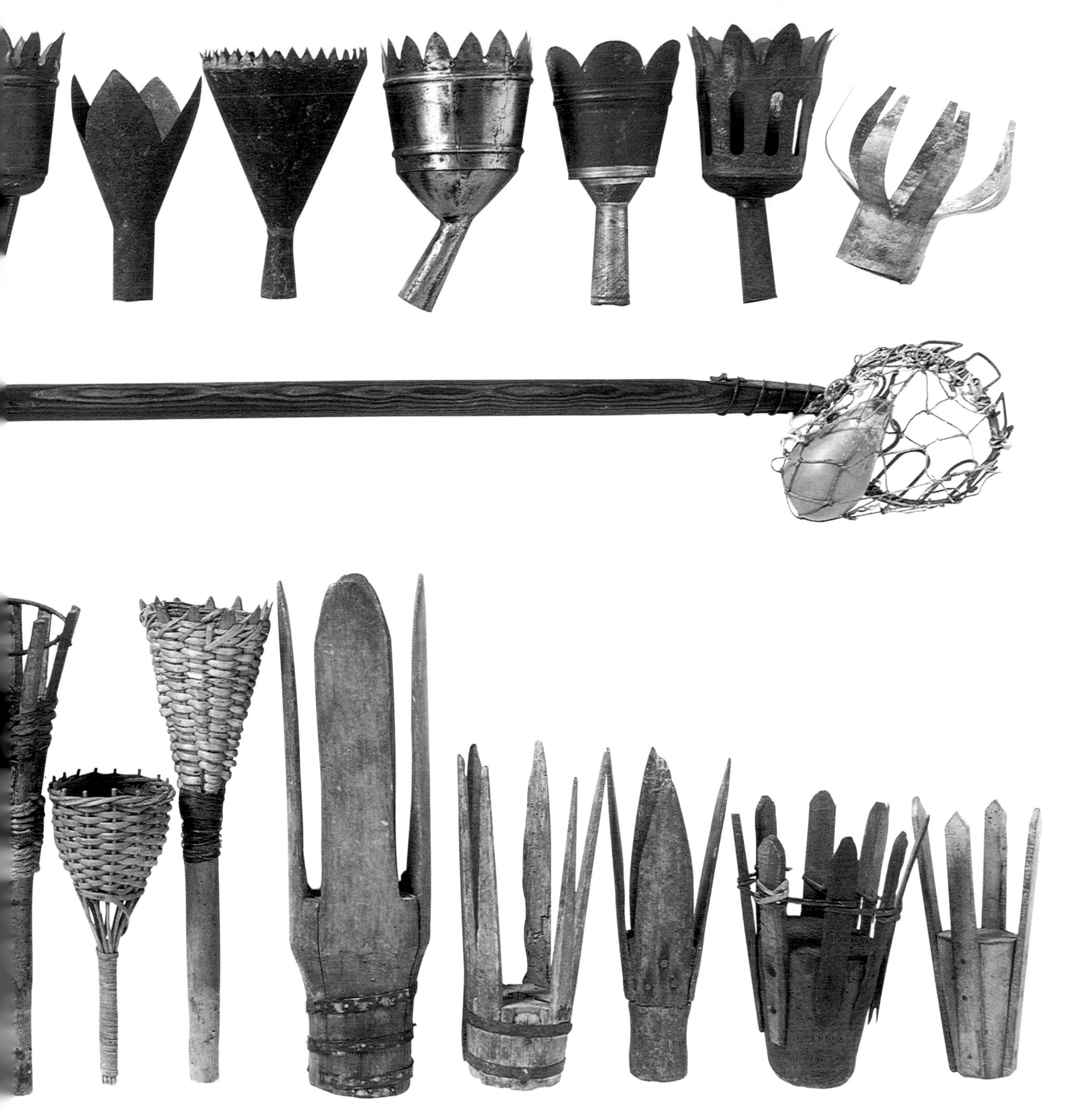

or fashioned out of recycled pieces of tin. Some were attached to long bamboo poles, while others came with canvas bags to catch the just-picked fruit.

ABOVE Wooden apple-picking baskets were worn around the neck. Their canvas bottoms opened easily so that the apples could be quickly emptied into larger containers.

RIGHT The tapered top of the three-legged wooden ladder allowed the picker to reach the highest pieces of fruit without damaging the branches.

LEFT AND RIGHT The harvesting of asparagus spears required a special tool that could reach and cut the vegetable's deep roots. Some asparagus knives, as they are called, had pointed and serrated sawlike heads, while others were rounded and sharp like carpenter's gouges.

In a fruit loft, apples are stacked on special graduated wooden shelves that assure adequate ventilation and offer a clear overall view of the condition of the fruits. As the room has to be kept dark, interior wooden shutters cover the windows.

ABOVE A special comb for collecting blueberries, which are too finicky to be picked by hand.

RIGHT Table grapes harvested in September could be preserved until Christmas by following the Thomery method. Each bunch of grapes, harvested with its stem, was placed in a glass jar filled with water and stored on specially angled shelves in a dark closet. The water was replenished as it evaporated, and a piece of charcoal in the jar maintained its purity.

A sampling of eighteenth- and nineteenth-century glass jars, all of which were enlisted in the Thomery method. The long, bottle-shaped

one, third from right, comes from England, where a similar method was adopted in the second half of the nineteenth century.

Competition with the
"EASY" LAWN MOWER
LAWN EASY MOWER
AT 10 A.M.
40 INCH "EASY" BEATS THEM ALL.
No 2. HALF AN HOUR LATER
"EASY"
LAWN MOWER

MOWING AND TRIMMING

Ever since nature first came under the gardener's care, its spontaneous growth has been undergoing transformation into sophisticated, sculptural creations. The basic structure and silhouette of the garden were determined by the contrast between flat, calm expanses, such as lawns, and the more elaborate groupings, shapes, and colors of flower beds, bushes, hedges, and trees.

In the Middle Ages open, well-maintained spaces for tournaments and war games were by necessity situated outside city walls. By the sixteenth century archery and jousting had been replaced by more peaceful activities, such as *boules*, or bowling, and *jeu de paume*, the ancestor of lawn tennis. The eighteenth century saw a dramatic change in scale; gardens now often featured canals, fountains, and allées and provided wide perspectives of beautiful green carpets that grew under the watchful eyes of numerous gardeners.

Wide, grassy areas were maintained with scythes; edges were cut with sickles; and more hard-to-reach places were clipped with wide-bladed sheep-shearing shears. The tools were sharpened at least three or four times a day on a small portable anvil or a whetstone, which was kept in a water box or sheath. The sheath hooked onto the gardener's belt and was held in place by a clump of grass. It was easier to cut the grass when it was damp from the morning or evening dew. The cuttings were either raked or swept before being fed to the animals or made into compost. Englishman Edwin Budling's invention of the lawn mower in 1830 would revolutionize lawn maintenance, assuring incomparable ease and evenness. By 1870 there were steam lawn mowers, and in 1902 the Ransome company introduced a lawn mower powered by a gasoline engine.

The clipping of trees and bushes was as important as the maintenance of grassy areas. While the Italians refined the art of topiary, creating perfectly clipped bushes in the shapes of columns, spirals, spheres, and pyramids, it was the French in the seventeenth century who gave all of Europe a taste for symmetrical garden compositions with their elaborate, geometrically patterned parterres, or flower beds, which were best appreciated from above.

Allées of hornbeams, yews, and linden trees were clipped into geometric shapes by gardeners standing on tall ladders or scaffolding and equipped with long-bladed shears or scythes tied to long poles. Trees were pruned and trimmed with articulated clippers. Because all of these tools were hand-forged, they came in a wide variety of shapes and weights. Blades and handles were often decorated; the heart was a favorite motif. Today electric power tools have replaced most of these tools. No longer in daily use, hand clippers and shears may have disappeared from the garden shed but often reappear as decoration on living room walls.

LEFT American Victorian-era trade cards extol the virtues of the new "Easy" lawn mowers. Even young ladies and dapper young men could operate the mower with little effort. Cutting a lawn was now child's play and no longer the gardener's chore.

PRECEDING PAGES Assembled in a wooden wheelbarrow are some of the basic, multipurpose tools necessary for the everyday maintenance of the garden: a spade, a rake, and a hoe.

ABOVE Hedge clippers came in a variety of shapes and sizes. The hand-forged iron blades could be wide or thin, long or short. Because of their weight, they required considerable strength on the part of the gardener,

who worked all day long, sometimes in acrobatic positions. The ingenious-looking double-bladed clipper, fourth from right, did not prove to be more effective than ordinary ones. The local blacksmiths who forged these sharp tools found it difficult to make the handles and blades proportionate—which explains the haphazard, rather ungainly look of some of the clippers.

The blades of many clippers were decorated with stars, hearts, leaves, the initials of the gardener, or the mark of the blacksmith. A screw allowed the blades to be tightened or loosened, or dismantled for sharpening or repair. The wooden handles were sometimes attached at an angle to the blades to make the gardener's stance more comfortable when he was clipping the sides of a hedge.

LEFT The mechanism of clippers with two rows of overlapping metal teeth derived from that of wheat-harvesting machinery. The long-bladed clipper with a double row of teeth resembling a sawfish, far left, is the only one that allowed the gardener to stand parallel rather than perpendicular to the hedge.

RIGHT Clippers with a parrot-beak-shaped head have always been used instead of saws for cutting low, thick branches. The head consists of a sharp blade and a hook that holds the branch steady. Both blade and hook pivot around a central axis and are held in place by a metal screw.

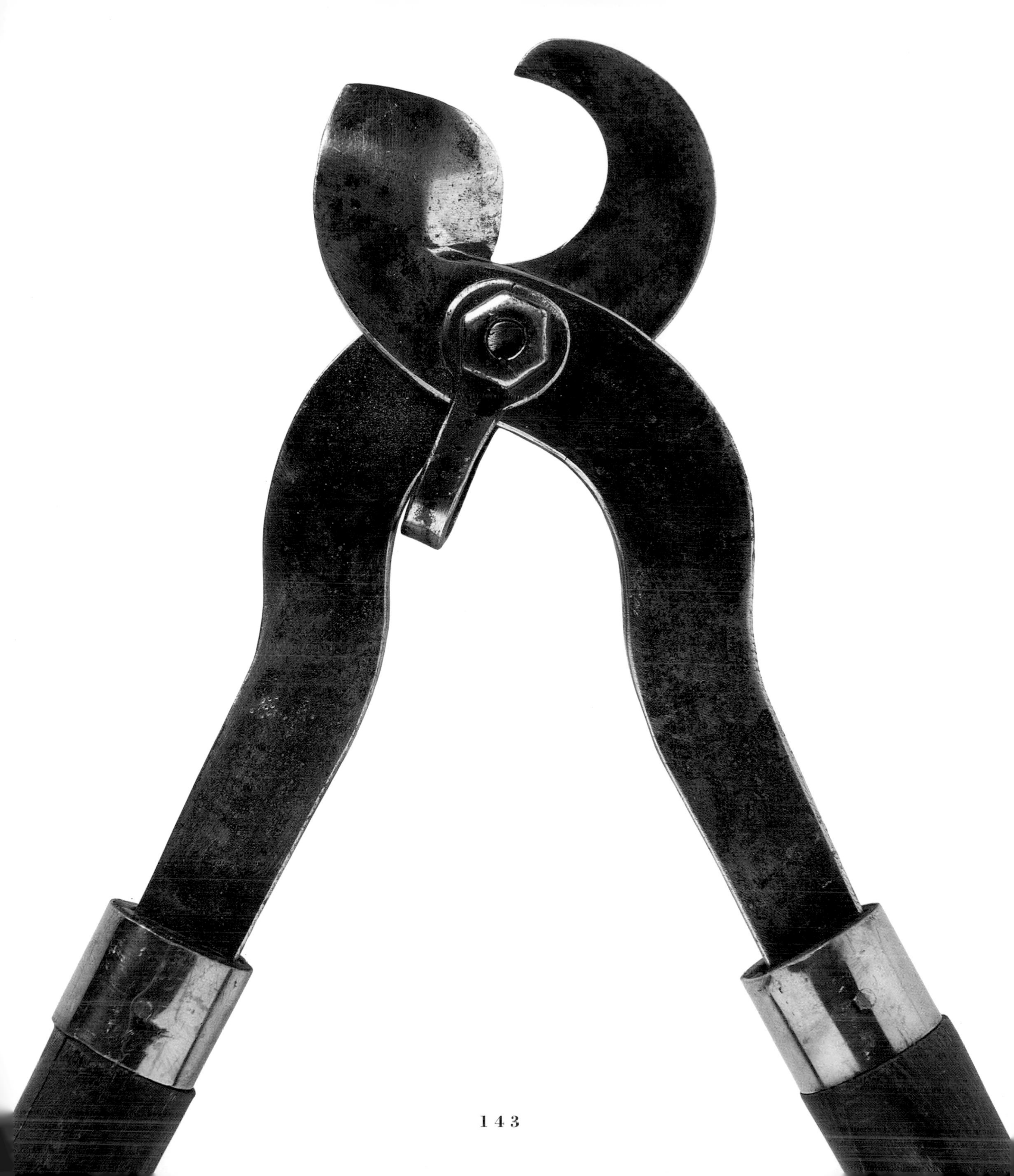

LEFT A group of frequently used tools includes an edging tool with a circular blade for lawn borders and flower beds; a fork for pulling out deep weeds; a long wooden spade for digging holes for young trees; and an unusually shaped wooden spade reinforced with metal.

RIGHT Graphically shaped iron tools, forged in the seventeenth, eighteenth, and nineteenth centuries, were for removing mistletoe from trees or cutting branches. Both sides of the tools were sharp so the gardener could cut or remove dead or undesirable branches by either pushing or pulling. The hooks enabled the gardener to catch branches as they fell.

BELOW The small, flat metal tool, second from right, removed mud from the gardener's tools or shoes. The other three probably date from the seventeenth century and were for pruning bushes and shrubs.

LD

RIGHT The lawn mower on wheels with spiral rotating blades was invented in 1830 by Englishman Edwin Budling, who derived its mechanism from a textile-cutting machine that evened the pile on velvet. The grass cuttings that did not end up in the mower's hood were swept into mounds before being taken to the compost heap.

BELOW Four specialized lawn-grooming tools, used in addition to the mower, from top to bottom: a grass plot–edging knife; a toothed roller to aerate the lawn; a long-handled vertical edging shear on a wheel for trimming grass at the edge of the lawn; and an eight-bladed cutter for achieving a perfect vertical edge.

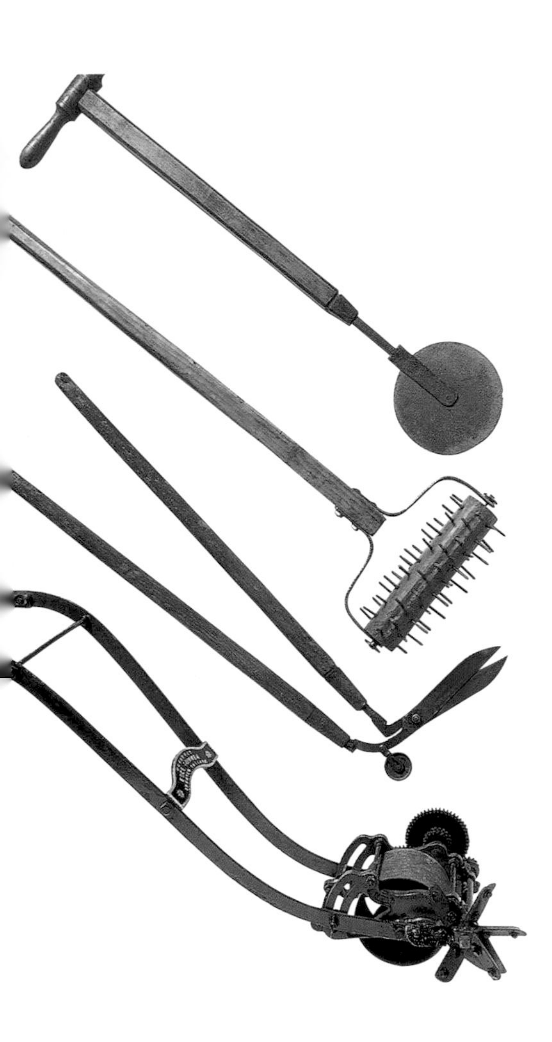

Sickles and scythes were not only made to suit the right- or left-handed gardener but also adapted to different tasks. The larger curved blades were for harvesting wheat or hay. The smaller blades were for the daily maintenance of the garden. The blade culminated in a straight piece of metal that was inserted into the wooden handle. Some handles were left in a rough state for a sure grip.

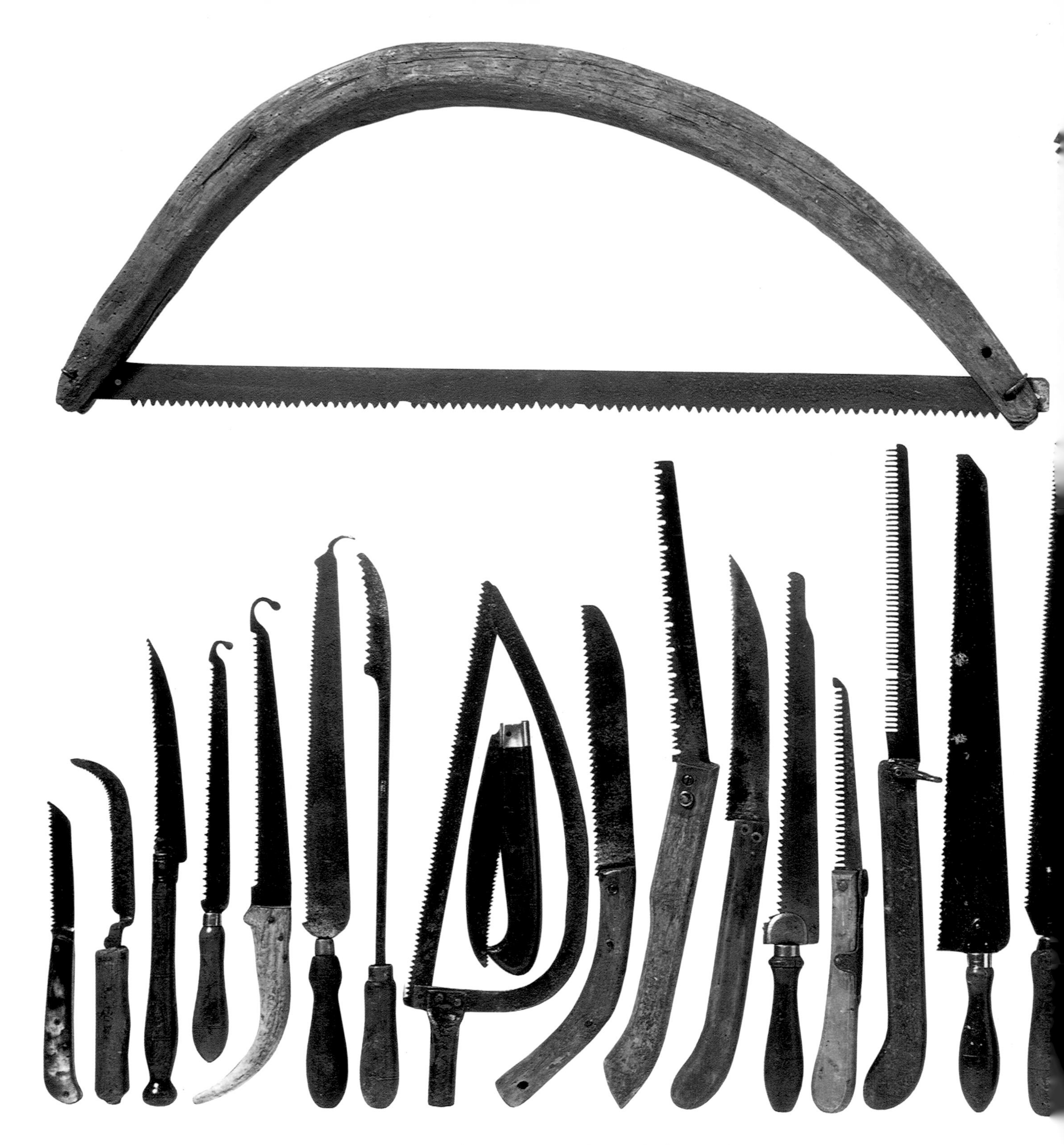

Saws were widely used in gardens, especially before the invention of pruners. Blades were fixed or folding, and handles were made out of a variety of materials, from wood to bull and stag horn. The simpler models were made by curving a thick but supple branch and attaching it to a

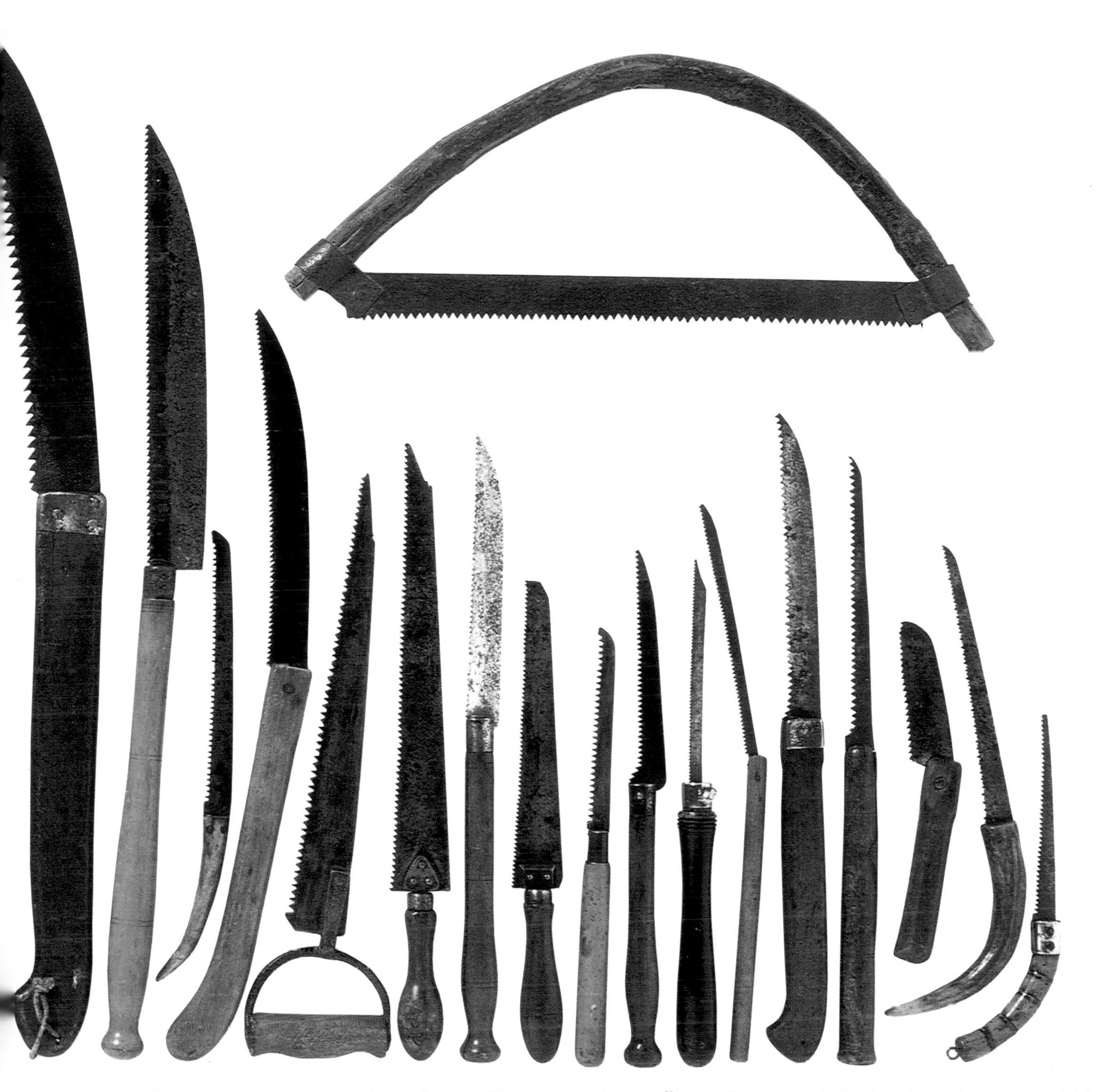

long serrated blade. Many saws were produced according to knife-making techniques. Rounded handles assured a good grip. The hooks at the end of the smaller saws helped catch falling branches and were also useful for hanging up the saws on nails in the toolshed.

A great variety of terra-cotta and sandstone plaques ornamented with raised designs and an array of decorative molded-metal elements that could be driven into the earth were available as stylish border markers.

DIRECTORY
BIBLIOGRAPHY
INDEX

Until recently, finding vintage garden tools often meant foraging through flea markets and combing antiques shows. But many antiques dealers are now specializing in garden ephemera, such as seed catalogs and old books, as well as in handmade garden tools and accessories, including rakes, spades, watering cans, sprinklers, cloches, and pruners. Listed below are sources in the United States, England, and France.

UNITED STATES

MARJORIE PARROTT ADAMS
34 Finn Road
Harvard, MA 01451
(508) 456-9102
Vintage seed catalogs, garden-related paper ephemera

ANCHOR AND DOLPHIN BOOKS
30 Franklin Street
P.O. Box 823
Newport, RI 02840
(401) 846-6890

L. BECKER FLOWERS
217 East 83d Street
New York, NY Zip TK
(212) 439-6001
Antique French bell jars

Vintage photograph of boy scouts and campfire girls learning to garden in Philadelphia.

MARILYN BRAITERMAN
20 Whitfield Road
Baltimore, MD 21210
(410) 235-4848
Antique books on landscape design

BUILDING ARTS
6515 75th Street
Cabin John, MD 20818
(301) 229-9307
Architectural remnants

DANOS & DANOS
240 Post Road East
Westport, CT 06880
(203) 227-0560

THE GARDEN ROOM
1179 Lexington Avenue
New York, NY 10028
(212) 879-1179

JOAN EVANS
Bucks County, PA
(610) 294-8153 / (610) 294-9192
Decorative architectural pieces

J. BARRY FERGUSON FLOWERS LTD.
P.O. Box 176
Oyster Bay, NY 11771
(516) 922-0005
Antique watering cans

BARBARA ISRAEL
(914) 232-4271 / (212) 249-1377
Call for more information

LEXINGTON GARDENS
1011 Lexington Avenue
New York, NY 10021
(212) 861-4390

JACK AND NANCY KIEFFER
3636 Cemetery Road
Hilliard, OH 43026
(614) 876-1383
Antique watering cans

THE MARSTON HOUSE
P.O. Box 517
Wiscasset, ME 04578
(207) 882-6010
Tools

MUNDER SKILES
799 Madison Avenue
New York, NY 10021
(212) 717-0150

POSTER AMERICA
138 West 18th Street
New York, NY 10011-5403
(212) 206-0499

RIVERBANK ANTIQUES
Wells Union Antique Center
Route 1
P.O. Box 3009
Wells, ME 04090
(207) 646-6314
Pots, measuring tools, sprinklers

ROOMS & GARDENS
290 Lafayette Street
New York, NY 10012
(212) 431-1297

DEBRA QUEEN
(508) 991-3106
Vintage flower pots, antique gardening books

LINDA & HOWARD STEIN
P.O. Box 11
Lahaska, PA 18931
(215) 297-0606

NANCY STEINBOCK
197 Holmes Dale
Albany, NY 12208
(800) 438-1577
Posters

TREILLAGE
418 East 75th Street
New York, NY 10021
(212) 535-2288
Garden-related furnishings, old terra-cotta pots

CECELIA B. WILLIAMS ANTIQUES
12 West Main Street
P.O. Box 319
New Market, MD 21774
(301) 865-0777

BRIAN WINDSOR
272 Lafayette Street
New York, NY 10021
(212) 274-0411

CHARLES B. WOOD III
P.O. Box 2369
Cambridge, MA 02138
(617) 868-1711
Antiquarian books on garden and landscape history

ROBERT L. ZIESMER
Antiques at Southwood
726 Woods Road
County Route 35
Germantown, NY 12526
(518) 537-4477
Bell jars

MAIL-ORDER CATALOGS

ASHWOOD BASKET CORPORATION
375 Union Street
Peterborough, NH 03458
(603) 924-0000
Baskets

GARDENERS EDEN
P.O. Box 7307
San Francisco, CA 94120-7307
(800) 822-9600
Pots, baskets, decorative accessories

GARDENER'S SUPPLY COMPANY
128 Intervale Road
Burlington, VT 05401
(802) 863-1700
New tools and equipment

HORCHOW
111 Customer Way
Irving, TX 75039

LANGENBACH
P.O. Box 1140
El Segundo, CA 90245-6140
(800) 362-1991
Garden tools

SMITH & HAWKEN
Mill Valley, CA 94941
"The Resource for Gardeners"
(800) 776-3336

ENGLAND

ALL OUR YESTERDAYS
Mal and Daphne Pearsey
North View
Pennyhill, Holbeach
Spalding, Lincolnshire PE12 8DN
01406 424-636

RACHEL BRAND
21 Kensington Place
London W8 7PT
0171 727-1151

THE DAVID BRIDGEWATER COLLECTION
Clifton Little Venice
London W9 2PX
0171 289 7894
Antique garden tools for sale

GEORGE F. CLARKE
Summerfields
Blackhole Drove
West Pinchbeck
Spalding, Lincolnshire
0177 564-0402

ANDREW CRACE DESIGNS
Bourne Lane, Much Hadham
Hertfordshire, SG10 6ER
0127 984 2685
Traditional plant labels

DRUMMOND'S OF BRAMLEY
Birtley Farm
Horsham Road
Bramley
Guilford GUS 0LA
Tel.: 01483 898-766
Fax: 01483 894-393

JUDY GREEN'S GARDEN STORE
11 Flask Walk, Hampstead
London NW3 1HJ
0171 435-3832

MARJORIE JAMES RARE BOOKS
The Old School
Oving
Chichester
West Sussex PO20 6DG
01243 781-354
Children's and illustrated books

THE LACQUER CHEST
75 Kensington Church Street
London W8 4BG
0171 937-1306

THE MUSEUM OF GARDEN HISTORY
Lambeth Palace Road
London SE1 7LB
0171 261-1891
Collection of garden tools

STEWART POTE
Bewerley House
Scarborough Road
Norton, Malton, New Yorkshire
YO17 8EF
Tel./Fax: 01653 692-055

GREG REDWOOD
Gardens Development Unit
The Royal Botanic Gardens
Kew, Surrey
0181 332-5543
Collection of tools and equipment

THE ROYAL HORTICULTURAL SOCIETY
80 Vincent Square
London SW1P 2PE
0171 834-4333
Reference library

SOTHEBY'S
Special garden sales
Summers Place
Billingshurst
West Sussex RH14 9AD
Tel.: 01403 783-933 / Fax: 01403 785-153

FRANCE

BOOKSTORES

LIBRAIRIE CART-TANEUR
Didier Cart-Taneur
11 bis rue Vauquelin
75005 Paris
Tel.: (1) 43 36 02 85 / Fax: (1) 43 31 86 02

LIBRAIRIE DU CAMÉE
François Clarenc
70, rue Saint-André-des-Arts
75006 Paris
Tel.: (1) 43 26 21 70 / Fax: (1) 43 29 38 88

POSTERS

ATELIER BRIGITTE BUSSIERE
Mounting, restoration, expertise
(by appointment)
43, rue de l'Arbre-Sec
75001 Paris
Tel.: (1) 47 03 32 58 / Fax: (1) 40 15 96 60

ATELIER LÉON KATCHIKIAN
Mounting, restoration, expertise
(by appointment)
Tel.: (1) 42 72 50 69 / Fax: (1) 42 72 05 22

SPECIALISTS

L'ATELIER D'ALBAN
10, rue Charles Legaigneur
78730 Sainte-Mesme
30 59 47 59

HUGUETTE BERTRAND
22, rue Jacob
75006 Paris
43 26 59 08

DANIEL BONITEAU
175, rue de Bourgogne
21410 Pont-de-Pany
80 23 67 22

COLLECTION PASSION
Jean-Claude Ayrault
52, rue Colbert
37000 Tours
47 61 05 56

JEAN-PAUL COMPIN
Marché Venaison
136, avenue Michelet
Allée 8, Stand 168
93400 Saint-Ouen
38 39 76 21

JOSETTE GOUBARD-HUBERT
1, rue du Maine
72200 Bazouges-sur-le Loir
43 45 20 30

ELSA HALFEN
14, rue des Jardins Saint-Paul
75004 Paris
(1) 48 87 13 54

L'HERMINETTE
Madame Leblic
4, allée Saint-Germain
Le Louvre des Antiquaires
2, Place du Palais Royal
75001 Paris
(1) 42 61 57 81

MARTINE HOUZE
5, bd Montparnasse
75006 Paris
(1) 45 66 79 85

JARDINS IMAGINAIRES
9 bis rue d'Assas
75006 Paris
(1) 42 22 90 03

JAMES JAULIN
By appointment
16 90 20 09 15

ISABELLE MALEVAL
Marché Dauphine
Boutique 23
140, rue des Rosiers
93400 Saint-Ouen
Tel.: (1) 40 12 87 36 / Fax: (1) 48 24 22 76

MICHEL R. MORIN
Marché Paul Bert
Allée 1, Stand 20
93400 Saint-Ouen
40 11 19 10

JEAN-CLAUDE PERETZ
1, rue Raspail
92300 Levallois-Perret
Tel.: 47 39 92 87 / Fax: 53 03 19 81

BIBLIOGRAPHY

Benoît, Fernand. *L'Outillage rural en Provence.* Editions Jeanne Laffitte Reprints, 1984.

Boitard, Pierre. *Les Instruments aratoires.* Paris: A. Ledoux Editeur, 1833.

Fussell, G.E. *The Classical Tradition in West European Farming.* Newton Abbott, England: David & Charles, 1972.

———. *The Farmer's Tools.* London: Bloomsbury Books, 1985.

Larousse agricole, 2 vols. Paris: Editions Larousse, 1921.

Morris, Alistair. *Garden Antiques.* Suffolk, England: Antique Collectors' Club, 1996.

Sanecki, Kay N. *Old Garden Tools.* London: Shire Books, 1987.

Thacker, Christopher. *Historic Garden Tools.* London: Museum of Garden History, 1990.

———. *The Genius of Gardening: The History of Gardens in Britain and Ireland.* London: Weidenfeld & Nicolson, 1994.

Trochet, Jean-René. *Aux Origines de la France rurale: Outils, pays et paysans.* Paris: C.N.R.S. Editions, 1993.

Velter, André, and Marie-Josée Lamothe. *Le Livre de l'outil.* Paris: Scandéditions, 1993.

ACKNOWLEDGMENTS

Getting *Everyday Things™: Garden Tools* into print has been an exciting and international endeavor between Paris, New York, and London. We have many people to thank in all of these places. They include: Marjorie Parrott Adams; Jacqueline and François Azan of Nacqueville Castle; Jonathan Bason of Vision Reproductions; Antoine Bernier; La Bibliothèque Forney; Jean-Claude Brisset; David Brittain; Jean-Paul Collaert of Societé Nationale d'Horticulture Française; Bruno Cousin; Andrew Crace and David Brown, who produced the plant labels throughout the book; Muriel and Bernard de Curel of St. Jean de Beauregard Garden; John Danzer of Munder Skiles; Philippe Druillet; Alice Eisen; Corinne Fossey, who first believed in this project; Laura Fronty; André Gayraud; Jean-Michel Gelly; Jean Hairon; Barbara Hogenson of the Barbara Hogenson Agency; Hardy Jones; Nicholas Kins; Jean Lefilliatre; Francine Legrand; Stanton Lovenworth; Béatrice and Guy Martineau; Gérard Nicod; Bertrand Painvin; Patricia and Bart Palmer; Sofia Parrenas; Paul and Eric Pellerin; Marie-Noëlle Pellerin; Jean-Marie Polydor and André Fleury; Patrick Portrait; Jean-Pierre Saint-Dizier; Matt Sarraf; Marc Schwartz and his assistant Yves Mery; Johnathan Scott; Michael, Jake, and Lucie Steinberg; Suttons Seeds Limited in London; Dr. Christopher Thacker; Kuldir Thandi; Brian Thompson; Pascal Trubert; Cléophée de Turckheim; Selma Weiner; and Abbie Zabar.

We are of course also indebted to our publisher, Abbeville Press. Our thanks to Robert Abrams, Mark Magowan, Patricia Fabricant, and Celia Fuller, but especially to Jackie Decter in New York and Marike Gauthier in Paris, two extraordinary editors who are also world-class diplomats. They have been with us every step of the way, and we will always be very grateful for their help and support.

INDEX

Page numbers in *italic* refer to illustrations.

PHOTOGRAPHY CREDITS

Copyright © Bibliothèque Forney: endpapers.
Copyright © Hubert Josse: pages 24–25.
Roy Miles Gallery, 29 Bruton Street, London W1/Bridgeman Art Library, London: page 58.

TROPHÉES